BEFORE THE YEAR DOT

BEFORE THE
YEAR DOT

June Brown

**SIMON &
SCHUSTER**

London · New York · Sydney · Toronto · New Delhi

A CBS COMPANY

First published in Great Britain by Simon & Schuster UK Ltd, 2013
A CBS COMPANY

1 3 5 7 9 10 8 6 4 2

Simon & Schuster UK Ltd
1st Floor
222 Gray's Inn Road
London WC1X 8HB

www.simonandschuster.co.uk

Simon & Schuster Australia, Sydney
Simon & Schuster India, New Delhi

A CIP catalogue record for this book
is available from the British Library

Hardback ISBN: 978-1-47110-182-3
Trade Paperback ISBN: 978-1-47110-183-0
eBook ISBN: 978-1-47110-185-4

Typeset in the UK by M Rules
Printed and bound by CPI Group (UK) Ltd, Croydon, CR0 4YY

Joy and woe are woven fine,
A clothing for the soul divine.

'Auguries of Innocence' by
William Blake, 1863

Oh, why should she who holds all my hopes of peace
Seek her peace with strangers
And increase the number of her failures?

Personal poem by
James Law Forsyth, 1948

Contents

Prologue

At sixteen I was very interested in palmistry. The fate line on my right palm had a distinct break at the age of thirty. It broke into two parts that ran for a quarter of an inch on parallel tracks. I used to look at it and wonder, 'What will happen to me when I am thirty that will change my life?' Of course, it was Johnny's death. But, in fact, my life was changed twice by death.

I can't remember a time when Marise wasn't there (she was sixteen months older than me).

'Junie, Junie, quick, get the cotton wool and the olive oil.' My sister Micie (my name for her, pronounced Meecie) woke me early one morning in June 1934. I was seven years old.

She was sitting up beside me in the bed that we shared in the big attic of our flat over Father's electrical business. The first floor had two main rooms – a drawing room and a dining room that seemed enormous to me. There was a kitchen, a bathroom and two bedrooms; one where my parents slept and the other where my father's canaries were kept in cages. They had had an aviary at our previous house in Warwick Road but the flat had no garden.

Micie and I were relegated to the attic, which, ironically considering Father's business, had no electric light and we had to go to bed by candlelight. I was scared whenever I was sent up into the darkness to fetch our nightdresses in order for us to be able to undress downstairs in the light.

The attic frightened me because there was a trap door set in the floor. It opened up to reveal a disused, back staircase, which would have led straight from the maid's attic bedroom to the kitchen, keeping her out of sight. We would wait in dread for this door to open, revealing some unknown terror.

I ran down the main staircase to the bathroom to fetch the olive oil and cotton wool – a panacea for earache. I did not think to wake my mother.

Micie was put into my parents' bed where Mother could care for her more easily. I wasn't aware that Micie was very ill. I can still see her sitting up in Mother's bed. I must have gone to say goodbye to her before I went to school. I have a memory of my granny going in to see her there and coming out saying, '*There* is a dying child', but, do I remember it or did Mother tell me long afterwards? I know I have a picture of it in my mind.

A few days later, I came home from school and Micie wasn't there. She had been taken to Ipswich General Hospital for a mastoid operation.

Rosebud (Rosemary, our younger sister) and I never saw her again.

My mother did tell me, much later, how dreadful it was to hear Micie cry out when the dressings packing the wound behind her ear were drawn out and then replaced. Whether an infection was introduced through this, I don't know, but Micie developed meningitis, became paralysed and, a few days later, she died. Had she lived, she would have been permanently paralysed and would have spent her childhood in one of those long, wicker spinal carriages. Yet, Mother, who was with her, said that, just before she died, she suddenly sat up in bed, held out her arms and smiled.

Micie was a very spiritual child. In the hospital, she had asked Mother to bring her Bible to her. In contrast, she was also a tomboy. I wasn't. I was timid.

I can't remember a time at all when Micie wasn't there. I can see myself at school outside the classroom door saying to my teacher, Miss Downing in a very ordinary, prosaic voice, 'Micie died yesterday.'

Her coffin lay in the darkened drawing room with the door closed. We never saw her, Rosebud and I. We just knew she was there.

On the day of the funeral, twelve-year-old Maggie Forsdyke had come to take care of us. She often used to come and play with us in the garden of our old house in Warwick Road and play our piano for us in the drawing room. Although she didn't know what the day was about, Rosebud, who was four, was aware of the atmosphere of misery and she started to cry. Rosebud didn't know why but she didn't want Maggie to play.

Micie was buried in the children's section of Ipswich Cemetery. She was buried in my brother John Peter's grave, who had died as a baby eighteen months before. She has a marble headstone, with angels on either side. Afterwards, we would walk to the cemetery to put flowers on the grave. In the winter, it was always chrysanthemums. I have never liked chrysanthemums since. Their smell reminds me. She and I had always shared a room, walked to school together and were hardly ever apart. Had she lived, we would have been in the same class at school, as I was to jump a class that summer, being clever as a child. Suddenly I was on my own. There was Rosebud, of course, but she was only four, and so was not much of a companion to me. She was a dear little girl but we were never as close as Micie and I had been.

Micie was born on the 6 October 1925, and died in June, 1934. Had antibiotics been available, there would have been no operation, she would not have died and, consequently, my life would have been quite different.

The loss of her affected my whole character and shaped the way I behaved for a long time. In particular, it influenced my expectations of men. Too dependent, I found it impossible to be happy alone. I was constantly in and out of love, always looking for the kind of caring that Micie had given me – the wholehearted acceptance of me just as I was. I kept looking for the friend I had lost.

I wanted to share everything as I had for the first seven years of my life. I found that companionship for a while, when I married my first husband Johnny. He was a great sharer and he did look after me and, in many ways, I looked after him.

I can be happy on my own now. I've learnt how to be.

Having written that I realise that I'm not being entirely truthful. After ten years of being a widow I would still like to share thoughts, laughter, meals, visits to the theatre, problems, house repairs! Not a husband nor a lover do I want. Just a compatible companion.

Chapter One

We moved very quickly after Marise's funeral to a semi-detached house in Grove Lane. Moving into this unfamiliar, gloomy house with its dark bare attics disorientated me further. It never seemed to feel or see the sun. Mother must have found the memory of Marise sitting up in her bed, seemingly not seriously ill and so soon afterwards lying in her coffin in the drawing room, too much to bear.

Micie's death hadn't drawn my parents closer either. Father was drinking heavily and there were many rows. Maybe that was partly caused by the accusation Grandma had flung at him the day that Micie died. Father arrived at Grandma's house, where we were staying, with the news of Micie's death. Grandma shouted at him, 'You killed that child.'

Apparently he had hit Micie round the head at some point

and, in Grandma's eyes, the blow to the head had caused the mastoid. Father rarely hit us. I remember him hitting me round the face only once when I had spilt a bottle of black ink on a white tablecloth; but that was some years later.

The Grove Lane house was the scene of constant arguments, which culminated one evening in an almighty row.

Rosebud and I cowered behind the sofa. Father seized the neck of Mother's black-and-white, semi-mourning dress – which belonged to her youngest sister, Auntie Marie – and the dress tore. Mother pulled on his tie in defence, almost throttling him.

Mother, Rosebud and I left Father the following day. That morning, once he had gone to his business and I had gone to school, Mother hired a van and removed our clothes and some of the furniture, taking them and Rosebud the short distance to her parents' house at 54 Spring Road. She met me from school that afternoon and took me back with her to Grandma's house.

Frightened of Father's reaction to this daylight flit, we promptly fled to Yarmouth, accompanied by Grandma.

The journey by steam train was an adventure for me. I had never been on one before. I remember holding my head out of the window to feel the wind rushing past and retreating with a smut in my eye.

It wasn't the most original hiding place. Ever since I could remember we had gone to Yarmouth for our week's summer holiday. But this time we were in constant apprehension that Father would follow. Everywhere we went, we would stop and peer round the street corners to make sure the coast was clear.

I have only one other memory of this time. We were hiding in a small, backstreet lodging house – quite different to our usual, respectable boarding house. Rosebud and I got up very early one morning to go down to the beach by ourselves where we thought the water would be much warmer if we walked into the path of the rising sun. Going to fetch our bathing costumes, which were in our private sitting room, we found our landlady, her husband and family using it as a bedroom. I remember them all suddenly sitting up as we opened the door. It was a very small house.

We went to the beach for our walk in the sea.

It was warmer.

Mother couldn't have known we couldn't swim, she wouldn't have let us go.

Towards the end of the week, Father appeared on the doorstep. I don't know how he found us he must have gone to Granny's house and asked where we were, dear grandfather, who would never lie, would have told him our hiding place!

Grandma opened the door to him. There was an altercation and Grandma, not in the least intimidated, knocked his pince-nez from his nose, which smashed into pieces. Nevertheless, when we returned to Spring Road the following day, we heard that Father had driven safely back to Ipswich without them.

Grandma's comment was, 'The Devil looks after his own!'

Chapter Two

We loved being at my grandparents' house in Spring Road and wanted to stay forever. The warmth and lack of arguments in the house were such a contrast to being at home with our parents. It was so peaceful. Grandfather Butler would sit in his high-backed wooden chair, in the corner of the sitting room, beside the fireplace and I remember his wireless, which sat on the shelf of the alcove cupboard on his left-hand side. This was run on square, glass batteries, called 'accumulators'. These had to be taken to the small garage on the corner of Alexander Road to be charged.

We would be sent to 'top up the accumulator'. We had to hold the batteries with great care, carrying them by their handles, keeping them upright, so that the battery acid didn't spill.

The garage we went to was owned by the Hayman family,

who lived in the house behind. There were several fair-haired sons and daughters, of whom I remember Dennis and Jessie most of all. Years later, Jessie wrote me a letter, full of all their news, after having seen me in *EastEnders*. I hope I answered it!

Grandfather was a kind, honest, upright man and he was extremely patient with Rosebud and me. We would sit on his knee, comb his hair and play with his heavy, gold watch chain and fob, which had a dark-red stone inset on one face and a jade stone on the other. He would take out his big, gold watch and teach us to tell the time. I still say five and twenty to one or five and twenty past two, as if I lived in another age.

Grandfather was named after his father, John Butler, who came over from Ireland as a young man to escape the horror of the potato famines of 1845 or 1846. He settled in the Soke of Peterborough, working as a farm labourer. Grandfather would tell us stories of his childhood in the thatched cottage in Orton Waterville, then a small village, on the outskirts of Peterborough. He would walk the four miles to school and back every day. The youngest of thirteen children, he was a bright boy and, by the time he was eight, he could read, write and do arithmetic, so he left school to work alongside his brothers in the fields.

One day, he told us he cut off the tip of his left index finger when he was using a scythe, picked it up, put it in his mouth to clean it, placed it back on his finger, wrapped it with his handkerchief and carried on working – he paid it no more attention.

He would show us the join – a faint ringed scar below the

nail, which grew in a ridged fashion from the damaged nail bed.

His English mother, our great-grandmother Ann Butler née Bell, was the village good-woman and midwife. While walking home late one night, after attending a confinement – this would have been some time in the 1850s – she passed an old woman, dressed in grey, wearing a poke bonnet. Ann said 'Goodnight' to her, the polite thing to do in the country, but there was no answer. Surprised at this, she turned, only to see the figure pass straight through the stone wall bordering the lane.

Grandfather had another ghost story which concerned the boot cupboard in the thatched cottage, one of a pair on either side of an open range. They had a friendly poltergeist, he said. They would hear the boots dancing away by themselves, clattering behind the cupboard door – a forerunner to *Riverdance*?

Our favourite of Grandfather's tales was about the runt of a litter of pigs which had to be reared indoors. It was kept warm in a box by the kitchen range. Grandfather said that pigs are very clean animals and that this little piglet would trot to the back door and squeal to be let out when it had a duty to perform.

We liked the idea of keeping a pig as a pet; we'd only ever had a dog and Father's canaries.

When Grandfather was older, he got a job in the 'big house' called Thorpe Hall, where he worked his way to the top of the hierarchy to become the butler.

His cousin, Annie, was the lady's maid. We went to visit Annie once when I was in my teens. She was in her eighties;

very well groomed with pretty, white hair. She told me that she would like to die, as she was very tired, but she couldn't 'go' before her husband, Alfred.

Their manners were impeccable, ingrained from years of service, and their lifestyle in their cottage was a microcosm of life at the 'big house'. Alfred would bring a jug of hot water to their bedroom every morning so that Annie could wash at the washstand before going downstairs. My mother remembered visiting them once when she was little and having a ride in a pony and trap.

Grandfather must have been ambitious as once he'd attained his position as butler at Thorpe Hall and could go no further, he left and went to work for the Great Eastern Railway (later, part of the LNER). He rose to be in charge of the main signal box at Mile End Road Junction.

It was while he was working there that he met my grand-mother who lived in the street where he had lodgings.

Grandma, Sarah Raphael, was very beautiful, with pale-blue eyes, perfect pale skin and black hair. She had been in love with the son of Lord Charrington – of Charrington's Brewery – but he was not allowed to marry her, as she was not considered good enough, or so we were told. Grandma's parents were Joseph Raphael and Louisa Wakeman. The Raphaels were originally Spanish Sephardic Jews who fled to France during the time of the Spanish Inquisition.

Another of the great-great-great-grandfathers from the Wakeman side was Isaac Bitton, a very famous bare-knuckle fighter in the East-End and also a Sephardic Jew.

He once went 74 rounds with an opponent on Wimbledon Common before winning the fight. He retired after that one!

One great-great-great-grandfather, or maybe even great-great-great-great-grandfather, was a famous French rabbi. My own great-grandfather, Joseph Raphael, settled in England in the East End of London. His wife Louisa's family are said to have come from Amsterdam, but her ancestors had arrived there from Algeria. My paternal grandfather came from Scotland and my paternal grandmother was supposedly of Italian stock.

I am a mongrel.

My grandfather was forty, and eighteen years older than my grandmother, when they met. She was the eldest of three sisters – Sarah, Dinah and Katherine, or Kitty for short. Dinah always said that Jack – as they called Grandfather – had really fancied her but that she was 'too lively for an old man'.

Although Grandfather Jack had come a long way since his childhood in Orton Waterville, his garden at Spring Road was set out in the same pattern as a village garden. One quarter of it was cut off from the rest by a trellis fence with a gate in the middle. This portion contained a small lawn and flowerbeds, which were encircled by a low fence. There was an outside lavatory across the path on the other side. Neat oblongs of torn newspaper, most probably cut from the *Evening Star* or the *News of the World*, were threaded on to a string, which hung from a nail beside the water closet. A built-in bench seat stretched from wall to wall, with a central hole.

Behind the lavatory was Grandfather's shed. His tools were always organised and arranged tidily. The rest of the garden was given over to neat rows of vegetables to the left of the central path, elder trees at the far end, fruit trees on the right and an enormous gooseberry bush which produced large red gooseberries each summer. We were only allowed through the gate into this part of the garden under Grandfather's supervision.

Life was more frugal at our grandparents' house. Their income comprised two pensions; one, the state pension, and the other, Grandfather's pension from the London and North Eastern Railway, or LNER.

Grandma made porridge with water, not milk – as at our house – and we had either bread with butter or bread with jam for tea – never both. Granny made her own cake – it always seemed to be one with caraway seeds. The biscuits were broken ones from Elmo's Stores.

There was no running hot water but the kettle was always singing on the hob of the little range in the back kitchen, although Grandma was modern enough to use a gas stove with an oven. There was no bathroom so we were washed in a tin bath in front of the range. Grandfather and Grandma slept in the middle bedroom. Rosebud and I shared the back bedroom with the gas mantel still attached to the wall, although Father had had the house wired for electricity. Father had bought the house for them to live in, with them paying a minimal rent which would have been enough to cover the mortgage. I loved going to bed there as there was the wonderful sound of ticking clocks. The one in my grandparents' room was a large wall clock with a pendulum. I still remember its sonorous tick-tock, tick-tock. Auntie Marie had the large front bedroom, and Mother must have intruded on her privacy and slept there with her.

Auntie Marie had been engaged for many years to Eric Jeffs, who eventually became our beloved uncle Eric. Uncle Eric loved motorbikes, and at this time he had one with a sidecar attached. He took Rosebud and me out in it, one at a time. It was an adventure to be put in this contraption, feeling special as if we were riding in a very fast pram. Uncle found the combination harder to manoeuvre than his solo motorbike, so sadly it didn't last very long. We were sorry; we liked that sidecar. But we cheered when he replaced it with a Dicky seat.

We must have stayed away from Father for several months, spending Christmas at Spring Road. It was that Christmas when I first realised what it meant – Micie being dead. Auntie Marie once told me that I would write notes saying, 'Dear Father Christmas, I don't want any toys, I just want Micie back.' Then I would put them on the fire and watch them flare and fly, as ashes, up the chimney.

Christmas had arrived and Micie didn't come back and I realised she would never be coming back. It was then, too, that I realised what death meant.

Auntie Marie told me that after Micie's death I became very withdrawn, a lonely child, and that Rosebud and I began to bicker. I wasn't used to being the eldest and having to be patient. You realise, when you have been the middle child and then become the eldest, just what a difference one's position in the family can mean. I had been sheltered by Micie; I wasn't expected to behave responsibly or look after the younger ones, so it was quite a shift for me of course I was the elder child then as Lois hadn't been born. I can remember bickering only once. We were trying to perform a spell to make a fairy in a thimble with a raindrop, a blade of grass, a spider's leg and a cobweb. We'd found the spell in an Enid Blyton book of fairy tales. We were squabbling over what to put in the thimble as a substitute for a spider's leg. Mother said, 'You'll never make a fairy if you quarrel.' We never did make our fairy.

Chapter Three

It was sometime in the New Year that Father turned to his own father, whom he hadn't seen for years, to help him persuade Mother to go back to him. Mother had agreed, reluctantly, to meet them at the Grove Lane house to discuss this away from the children.

My mother Louisa, née Butler, was born in 1899 though she always said she was born in 1900. My Auntie Lottie told me just after my mother had died that it was she who was born in 1900; my mother hadn't liked the idea of being born in the nineteenth century. She'd gone to London after an unhappy love affair with a man whom she discovered was already married.

She left Ipswich to take a job in a milliner's salon, making hats, living in digs in Balham. On a visit home to see her parents in Ipswich one weekend, unfortunately, she met my father who lived in London but had come to visit his friend Sir Percy Bostock.

Father was staying at the White Horse Hotel, the best hotel in Ipswich. And so they met.

Everything had begun to go wrong for my father since his unwise move in taking out a court action against one of his customers to recover money owing to him but left unpaid. At the time my father owned the well-established firm of Wood & Co, Electrical Engineers. Father knew nothing about electricity except how to change a light bulb and mend a fuse. He should have been an estate agent – he was fascinated by empty houses. I was, too, funnily enough.

He lent his friend from the rich days – Sir Percy Bostock – £200 to start an estate agency in London which prospered. Father's big mistake was in not joining him in this venture, but buying instead an electrical business of which he had no knowing. When Father's customer failed to pay, Father should have had the sense to forego the debt and keep the other members of 'the gentry' as his clients. His action caused them to withdraw their custom in support of one of their own and his business fell away.

He had to move the business to Number 13 Great Coleman Street, a less-favoured position, and the family went with him as there was a two-floored flat above it, Number 13A which saved Father from having to pay rent on Number 50 Warwick Road, the house where we'd been so happy.

We had to dispense with Ruby, our maid, our dog Chip, Micie's Fairy Cycle; Father's aviary; and the large dining-cum-billiards table.

Grandfather Brown arrived, heavily swathed in a cap and muffler against the chill of the wind, having been driven down by his youngest son, father's half-brother Bertram, in his open-topped sports car. They were rather posh. Grandfather's second wife had been what Mother called 'one of the Lamploughs'.

She did not have fond recollections of her father-in-law. During a visit to his house on one occasion before she and Father were married he had picked up a pair of scissors and cut off her long red fingernails.

Mother finally agreed to a reconciliation, though, on the condition that Father give up drinking and sign the Temperance Pledge. He did so.

I know now that Mother was more influenced by the fact that Auntie Marie didn't want us living with them any longer. When I was older and Mother was grumbling about Father's behaviour yet again, I, losing patience with her, said, 'You never should have gone back to him. We should have stayed with Grandma.' She answered quite vehemently, which was very unlike her, 'I know you think an awful lot of your auntie Marie, but she didn't want us there!'

Apparently Marie had said to Mother, 'You should go back to your husband where you belong.' We loved her and her fiancé Uncle Eric but clearly she liked her peace when she came home from work without having two little girls demanding her attention.

Perhaps she didn't want Mother there because Mother was the favourite daughter. She was the one who was amusing and bright, attractive, could sing and play the piano and whom everybody loved. I think maybe Auntie Marie was a bit jealous. But then again, I was frightened of her dog, a rather large black one called Nigger that used to jump up and bark and there had been talk of his being given away because of me – with our leaving, she was able to keep him.

Unwillingly, Rosebud and I were once more in that gloomy house in Grove Lane. But at least Father was sober and there were no more rows. We started to go out as a family.

Mother and Father would take Rosebud and me to a small pub in a backstreet nearby called the Buck's Horns, where Father would drink grapefruit juice.

Rosebud was a dainty little thing and extrovert; she could do a wonderful Mae West impersonation and at the pub they'd say, 'Rosebud, do Mae West!' She'd stroll up and down with her hand on her hip, with her headful of blonde ringlets and her tip-tilted nose, saying, 'Come up and see me sometime.'

I sat and watched. Rosebud was familiar with all the American filmstars: Mother was in the habit of taking Rosebud with her to the cinema in the afternoons while I was at school, so she learnt all the phrases and mannerisms from the Hollywood films.

We were less keen on the winter walks we did as a family. Taking the trolleybus to Wherstead we'd walk along the Strand which was the river path on the south shore of the Orwell. A chill wind would be blowing off the water, and we'd walk for what seemed miles, then thankfully turn round and walk back, calling in at the pork butcher's shop as we reached the trolley bus stop to go home. As you can imagine, this butcher only sold pork chops, tenderloin, joints, sausages, brawn, and Chitterlings, which Rosebud and I wouldn't touch once we knew they were pigs intestines. We'd walk in the bare, muddy fields, we liked summer meadows but not muddy fields.

When we got home I wasn't happy to be at the house, although it was warmer, it felt cold and silent. Mother didn't play the piano nor sing any more. Rosebud and I would read our story books or play with our dolls for company. No visitor ever came to Grove Lane.

One Sunday afternoon however we took a trip to visit Mother's great-uncle and -aunt – Montague and Dorothy, or Monty and Dolly – to see their new bungalow in Costessey, a suburb of Norwich. Aunt Dolly looked rather like a parrot – she had Marcel-waved hair dyed auburn, a very high colour and a small beaky nose. She found her husband intensely amusing. 'Oh, Mont, you are a fool!' she'd say affectionately, in her Norfolk accent. She was very smart and wore very good clothes: fur felt hats and fine leather shoes. Outdoor shoes had to be removed by everyone when they entered the bungalow. She was excessively houseproud. Their lawn was a bowling green, as Uncle Monty liked to play bowls.

I remember clearly Uncle Monty's driving habits. On the two-way road to Felixstowe he would recklessly overtake every car until he reached the head of the line, then he would chug along at twenty miles an hour, much to the irritation of the queue of cars behind him! He was a lovely man – apart from that – always laughing. He was one of Mother's Jewish uncles. He was tall and broad with wide cheeks and a large beaky nose and twinkling eyes. We had a Toby jug that Mother had bought from a second-hand shop that looked exactly like him. Mother loved rummaging around in second-hand shops and coming home with 'treasures', a passion that I have inherited.

When we got to Monty and Dolly's, they made a great fuss of Rosebud. She was encouraged to show them her Mae West impersonation – 'Rosebud, do Mae West!' When it came to our going back home, Aunt Dolly said, 'Let Rosebud stay for a week.'

And so I returned with Mother and Father, sitting alone in the back seat of Father's car. Forty miles home, in the dark, and not a word was spoken to me.

They knew I was still very affected by Micie's death, but people weren't concerned with psychology then. Perhaps it was better because you learnt to survive without sympathy.

I returned to Grove Lane with no sisters at all, to go upstairs to bed alone with no one to talk to. I was on my own. I have never felt such intense loneliness as I felt then. I still remember it as if it were yesterday.

Chapter Four

I longed to be back at Warwick Road in our old house. I wanted to be playing in the garden with Micie, swinging in the hammock slung between the pear and apple trees, opening the door to the greenhouse in the summer to savour the slightly bitter but intriguing smell of the leaves of the tomato plants, standing in rows with their clusters of red fruit.

I wanted our friend Maggie, our nice maid Ruby and Mummy playing the piano in the drawing room with us around her singing the 'Indian Love Lyrics' – her favourite songs. I tried to copy her warm, rich soprano voice, which made me sing in my throat. I had to learn not to when I was older.

I wanted to be sleeping in a bed with Micie, going to school together and being taken to Miss Tracey's kindergarten by Annie, our first maid, where I remember learning to count on the abacus and to knit with big wooden needles and thick cotton thread that didn't break. Once, when Micie had started school, I sat on the stairs knitting by myself, watching my parents clear out the box room ready for the new baby – not yet born.

At Christmas time in Warwick Road, we would have Christmas trees that reached to the ceiling and pretty lights that Daddy brought home from his business – a row of painted Chinese glass lanterns that you had to be careful not to break. Daddy put the lights on the tree and plugged them in. If one lantern didn't work he would put a little piece of silver paper in it and it lit up. It was like magic.

We had presents on the tree as well, because that's where my black dolly was, at the top of the tree next to the fairy.

We made paperchains, sitting at the kitchen table with Ruby – long strips of coloured paper: pink, yellow, red, green and blue. We'd put glue on a brush and stroke it on to the ends of each strip, then join them into a circle, one looped through the next, and when the chain was long enough.

Daddy fixed them to criss-cross the room under the ceiling with beautiful fold-out coloured paper bells attached.

Mummy would always give us a Christmas party. Micie asked a girl from her class once and she said it was the best Christmas party she'd ever been to. Mummy worked so hard: there'd be a cake, sweets, chocolate, fruit and nuts, jellies and trifle and loads of things to eat and lots of things to do. She thought it was marvellous.

We played games, with Mummy playing the piano for Pass the Parcel, Musical Bumps and Musical Chairs. Once, one of the girls was pushed off a chair but she didn't hurt herself – and everyone had a present to go home with.

In the evenings sometimes Daddy made the big oak table into a billiards table with its winding handle and they would play – he showed mother, sometimes, where to hit the ball so that it went into the pocket or 'in-off'.

On Christmas morning we would wake up really early and find piles of presents at the foot of our beds, plus a stocking containing a tangerine and some nuts in shells. We didn't go to church on Christmas morning – we listened to the radio – and the Christmas meal was always a very big occasion.

One year when Mother had made the Christmas pudding back in August, the suet was off, but of course, we didn't find out until Christmas Day! Mother was a very good cook, though, and she loved to do it. Christmas dinner was an opportunity for her to show off her talents – turkey, Brussels sprouts, potatoes, carrots, parsnips, stuffing, bread sauce and sausage meat. She was an efficient cook, too – unlike me – and dinner would always be ready for 1.30 p.m.

Father would carve the turkey and pour the brandy over the Christmas pudding and light it.

He would make us cocktails to drink on Christmas Day, too, which we would have in tiny liqueur glasses. Occasionally Mother would give us some of her morning Guinness. It wasn't forbidden so we were used to it.

Micie and I were very alike. She was only sixteen months older than me and we both had round faces, with big eyes, short, dark, bobbed hair and fringes. There is a photograph of

us with me sitting on my little wicker armchair in the garden
and Micie is standing beside me, trying to make me laugh by
scratching her bottom. It is impossible to tell the difference
between us. I just know who is who because I can remember
Mother taking the photograph with her Box Brownie.

A year later, Micie's face had thinned down a little and
she had started to wear her fringe clipped to one side. She
had also grown taller, so it was easier to tell us apart.

She was a very bright child. Already talking at sixteen
months when I was born, she asked Mother's live-in mater-
nity nurse, 'Nursie, may I have a mappy for my dolly?'

Maggie Forsdyke, who lived near, was twelve when Micie
died. She was wonderful with us. She was like an older sister
and a nursemaid. She loved us and was always with us in the
garden.

We liked her because she liked us and she was a very imaginative child who used to draw us into rather exciting games.

At our bedtime she'd sit by our bed and make up stories as
we drifted off to sleep. She didn't always finish them – I think
sometimes she ran out of inspiration or we fell asleep, but
she kept us enthralled and mystified.

One day, in the garden at Warwick Road, Maggie decided
that we were going to do a play – well, several plays really.
'We'll act this fairy tale,' she said. 'Then, we'll do this one. Oh,
and we'll do that one – and we might as well do that one as
well.' We found acting rather embarrassing and were reluc-
tant, but if Maggie said we were going to do it, we did it.

I think Maggie liked directing and telling us what to do –
and this was going to be a public performance! I can see
Mummy standing at the side garden door, with scissors and

a roll of blue crêpe paper from which she was going to make our costumes.

The only time I was ever cross with Micie was during our theatrical performance in the garden. We had pinned a notice on the back gate, which was next to the front of Maggie's house. The entrance fee was a ha'penny.

In the interval, we had gone down to the corner shop to get refreshments for the audience and we also bought two oranges to share between the performers. Micie cut them up and distributed them to the audience as well – that's why I was grumpy with her.

Micie didn't care about keeping anything for herself.

I have this impression of her: always kind, loving and caring, never nasty. If she had been, I would remember, for those are the moments that stay strongly in the mind. She looked after me. I adored her – I didn't realise it at the time, but I did.

Once, Micie and I were waiting for a trolleybus in Spring Road.

We were between maids at the time – our last maid, Sylvia, had been sent home after a week. She was so homesick, she cried all the time, and was returned to her father's farm!

The first trolley to appear was a new double-decker, one of the first of its kind in Ipswich in 1932. I was frightened by it and didn't want to get on – I was five. Micie would have loved to run up the stairs and sit at the front, but instead she took my hand, stood back and waited patiently until the single-decker trolley came along. She had such a kind, generous nature.

In fact, after she died, Mother would say, 'She was too

good to live', which was often said about someone who had died young, but in Micie's case I think it was true.

I trusted Micie implicitly. I did anything she suggested in 'follow my leader' fashion, even quite daredevil things. Micie was the daredevil, I wasn't. She would often put me on the rear carrier of her Fairy Cycle and we'd go shooting off down Bellevue Road, a hill close to our house, then straight over across Alexandra Road which formed the crossroads at the bottom of the hill. Fortunately, in those days there wasn't much traffic, so we never had an accident, but it was lucky, all the same.

On one occasion, I didn't stay close enough to her and came to grief.

There was a vast horse-chestnut tree near to where we lived and we would pass it while walking home on our safe side of the road. It dropped big shiny conkers as far across as the opposite pavement. I couldn't resist running across the road to gather some extra-large ones from the gutter. Micie saw me from the other side and called, 'Junie, come back.' I started to cross, but although I heard a cycle bell ringing and turned to look, I saw nothing.

Suddenly, I was being dragged, face down, between the front and back wheels of a bicycle that had been speeding down the hill from the top of Spring Road. I ended up opposite the Scout hut, just before the Ipswich-to-Felixstowe viaduct.

My knees were utterly scraped, red-raw and bleeding. I had no other injuries, I must have held my head, hands and feet up in the air. My legs would have been bare but for little white ankle socks and button-up brown leather shoes. The man on the bike walked me and Micie five minutes down the road to my grandma's house. He didn't think to put me on the saddle and wheel me there – perhaps he was too shocked. I imagine my dear grandfather would have bandaged my knees.

The only other memory I have of the incident is being made to stand on the dining-room table by my father and being firmly told to straighten my legs, while I cried because it was so painful.

The bandages stayed on for a month and I walked all the time with my knees bent. The weight on my feet weakened them, my arches fell and my slim, straight feet were gone for ever.

I have hated them ever since, and would dig my toes into the sand to hide them when photographs were taken on the beach. My first husband, Johnny, used to say they were pretty but he was just being kind! I expect poor Micie got the blame for it, yet she would have only been six, coming up to seven.

Micie and I had empathy for each other. One night Father came home a bit merry with two presents: a slightly used box of Reeve's paints in china dishes and a large chocolate rabbit with a blue ribbon around its neck. He gave me the paints – I was his favourite at the time – and Rosebud got the choco-late rabbit. Having taken the ribbon from its neck, he gave this to Micie. As with the trolleybus when she had sensed my fear, I knew just how Micie must have felt at that moment. I wasn't pleased to have the paints, I could only think of how unfair it was to Micie.

I don't think Father was very fond of her. Perhaps he was jealous of my mother's affection for her. She was her first-born and Mother was very attached to her. When Father died, Mother gave me her marriage certificate as I was registering his death for her. I wondered why she looked at me oddly but said nothing. It was only when I was assembling the birth, marriage and death certificates after she had died herself a year later that I realised the meaning of her expression. The date of her marriage certificate was 8 August 1925, Marise's birth was 6 October 1925 – two months later. Micie must have been a very endearing baby because Mother told me that she heard Micie crying while she was in labour with me and jumped out of bed to go to her, having to be stopped by a nurse.

Mother had a very good way with children. She would let us learn from experience. I was given some valuable lessons. When I dropped my poor little naked celluloid dolly, with her holes at the top and bottom of her hollow body where the arms and legs were hooked on to the elastic band inside her, into the water butt outside the greenhouse to see if she could swim, nobody hoisted themselves over the edge and rescued her from her watery grave.

I didn't know she'd fill with water and drown when I put her in for a swim! I learnt that day that if you fill a hollow object with water it will sink – unless it's a boat!

After Micie started school, I was in the garden playing on the ground – it was a sunny day. Mother had given me two halves of an orange and the glass orange squeezer to make myself a glass of juice. I had pressed the juice happily out of the second half, poured it carefully into the glass and was just about to drink it when a hand came from nowhere and swept the glass away.

'Oh! You can't drink that.' And off went Mother with my lovely orange juice – now a dirty shade of grey-brown.

It was then that I realised I should have washed my hands. Mother didn't take me to wash them, nor did she give me another orange, a second chance.

I didn't whine, I didn't say anything; I just watched as my juice disappeared. If you made a mistake you had to live with the consequences.

The Christmas before I was given a black baby doll that I'd longed for. She sat at the very top of the Christmas tree. I slept that night with her on the pillow beside me and in the morning she woke up with a white cheek and I with a black one. What did that teach me? I wonder. 'We're all the same under the skin.' 'You can't judge a book by its cover', or just buy the best – cheap things don't last! All I know is, I wasn't given another one. My paint washed off but dolly's face stayed white. Mother's way of bringing you up let you work things out for yourself. She didn't put herself on a pedestal so she was saved from falling off.

Mother was always very pretty. She wore her hair in 'ear-phones', as I mentioned earlier – plaits of reddish-brown hair, wound round and pinned over each ear, with a fringe in front. She had been very beautiful. She had a slim, straight nose until Father, who had been drinking that evening, drove his 'open tourer' into a milestone and Mother was thrown forward into the car windscreen.

They were on their way home to The Hollies in Creeting St Mary, where we had lived before Warwick Road. Mother had fourteen-month-old Micie on her lap and was seven months pregnant with me. As a result, her nose became shorter and blunter, with a small scar like a fingernail impression on the bridge. When I was in my teens I dug my fingernail into my nose and said, 'Look, Mummy, I have a scar, just like you.' Mother, being gullible, was completely taken in, until I laughed – then she did, too.

Mother was very warm but not physically demonstrative, and I only once recall her treating me affectionately, after she had dug the scissors slightly into my neck while cutting my hair. She picked me up and held me in her arms to comfort me. She could also seem remote. At times she could be caught staring into the distance and when we were older we would we would snap our fingers before her face to bring her back! After Mother died, Auntie Lottie said that she had been a very affectionate girl but that her marriage had changed her.

Mother was very good with her needle and always made our clothes. She never used patterns.

Once when Micie and I were going to be in a school concert, she spent hours making two tobacco-coloured velvet dresses, smocking the waists and embroidering their pointed collars. (We always dressed alike.) Micie and I trotted proudly off to the concert rehearsal with Ruby. On arrival, the teacher said, 'Oh, those dresses are far too sombre. Haven't you got anything lighter?'

Next day, Mother dashed out and bought us each a dress of artificial silk. Fashion was still influenced by the Twenties so they were absolutely straight with dropped waists and weren't nearly as nice as our handmade dresses.

She was also a dab hand at renovation. She had a grey squirrel coat which became a grey squirrel jacket, then a grey squirrel cape and finally, a grey squirrel collar! Violets smelt wonderful then, and Mother always wore them pinned on to her grey squirrel.

Working with fur is quite difficult, as you have to cut it from the back with a razor blade and oversew each piece. It's not something that one can just 'run up on the Singer' – we adopted that expression at drama school in 1948 when Dior's new look was in full swing. One of the students, Moira, had a mother who made all her clothes. Her 'New Look' designs always outdid ours. I remember one suit in particular, which had a spectacularly full skirt and layers of stiff petticoats. Moira was reputed to have said, 'Oh, Mother ran it up on the Singer.' The expression became a catch-phrase and my girls have inherited my mother's ability to run things up on the Singer!

Until I was seven, Mother always had a general maid to help her in the house and walk us to school. Father paid the bills and looked after the finances and Mother did as women did in those days: she looked after the house. Out of her housekeeping she bought herself things, not a great deal – she wasn't extravagant – but she bought her toiletries, her clothes and material to make ours. She also managed to save.

When we had a maid, Mother's housekeeping allowance was £2 15s (£2.75) a week. Some people only earned that as a week's wage, so Mother's housekeeping allowance was quite generous. It is amazing to think how far this money stretched to cover food for the whole household and the maid's wages of ten shillings (50p) a week. The maid lived in, so the money was hers to spend as she liked.

Mother went to a registry office to find her maids, who

were mostly young girls from the country, usually farmers' daughters. I always get cross when people talk about getting *married* in a registry office. A registry office was where you found a register of people who wanted to work in domestic service. A register office is where you get married.

It wasn't as if Mother sat on her bottom. She always helped the maid do the housework. In the morning they would do it together; the beds were made – sheets and blankets are much more time-consuming than shaking a duvet. Then there was the hoovering, dusting and polishing. Mother did all the cooking. We weren't made to work hard as children but we were shown how to do housework. Mother taught us to cook, not that I've ever been much of a culinary genius. My own children preferred processed beef burger and fish fingers to my beef stews or steak and kidney puddings.

I remember our last maid Ruby most clearly. She was probably only about eighteen but she seemed older to me, as a small child. She had dark-brown hair and eyes and she lived with us in Warwick Road. She had a room at the back of the house. Through Ruby I learnt very early on that it was unwise to make personal remarks. One day she was standing at her dressing-table mirror doing her hair and I was beside her, watching. I could see dark hair on her upper lip and, looking up at her, I said, 'Ruby, why have you got a moustache?' I knew men had moustaches but I didn't know girls did. Ruby didn't answer – she just gave me a look. Her look has stayed with me all my life.

We always holidayed in Yarmouth, and loved our times there. Yarmouth, with its donkey rides along the sands, and the man who walked along the beach with his tray, calling out 'Noogaar!' with a mock French accent and 'Ripe Williams!' (pears). We loved the board walkways up the sands that led to the little huts by the promenade selling ice-cream and trays of tea, one of which we would buy to take back to Mother, sitting in her deckchair, always fully clothed, guarding the beach paraphernalia. We would paddle in the sea and make sandcastles with moats for the tide to fill and then wash the castles away. If it was very hot, Father would dig us a hole in the sand, with seats formed in the walls. We could sit down there in the cool damp sand.

As a special treat, Father would pay for us to take a trip out to sea in one of the many rowing boats that vied for trade along the shore. On rainy days we'd wander around the arcades, put pennies in the machines or try to get ping-pong balls into the mouths of clown heads as they turned from side to side. We'd try to lift the prizes with the grabber cranes, but we only ever caught dolly-mixture sweets.

There was a Punch and Judy show, which we loved to watch, frightened by the crocodile and amused and horrified by the antics of Mr Punch, as he thwacked and squawked. We'd throw pennies on to the blankets laid out beside the elaborate models carved by the sand artists below the promenade. We'd wish that we could take a ride in the horse-drawn carriages that clip-clopped along the lower road but they were too expensive.

A business associate of Father's, a Mr Guyton, once took us all on a day trip to Yarmouth in his Opel car. We took tea at the rather smart Sheiling Hotel and packaged up the leftover cakes to feed to the horses that pulled the carriages on the Lower Road. Then we went on to Gorleston, where we had the most wonderful ice-cream made with real strawberries and cream and served in little silver bowls. It was so rich that I could only eat half of it.

A boy was born into our family in the snowy January of 1932, shortly before I turned five, but he died sixteen days later from pneumonia. His name was John Peter; I don't know if he was actually christened. I don't remember a clergyman coming to the house, only the constant activity of the nurse up and down the stairs and in and out of the back bedroom with steam kettles, moist air to help the baby's breathing. There was no other treatment then. Mother blamed the nurse for taking him out in the pram in the cold when he was only a week old.

The nurse left when John Peter died, and Annie, our maid, then came back to us. Annie sent me up a day or so later to ask Mother for money for the milkman who'd called at the back door, and I stood beside her bed as she sat propped up on the pillows, crying.

I was bewildered. I'd never seen her cry. I never saw her cry again – not even after all the other deaths, Micie, Uncle Eric, Grandma and Granddad, all of whom she loved dearly – until the day of my father's funeral in the car on the way to the cemetery; and him she didn't love.

Mother revealed to me, when I was much older, that Father had been having an affair during this pregnancy. She had found out and confronted him. Father became quite belligerent and aimed a kick at her stomach. In those days one wouldn't have known the sex of the baby – perhaps he might have behaved differently if he had known she was expecting a son.

Despite Father's drinking and Mother's sadness when John Peter died, I loved my childhood in Warwick Road. I sometimes wish I could go back and live there again. The photograph of us three girls and Father walking up the beach at Yarmouth encapsulates it for me. I have the framed photograph sitting on the hearth in my sitting room, and I look at it and think how free and open we look – secure – before Marise died.

Chapter Five

Sometime that summer of 1932 the Templeys came to stay –
Auntie Lottie, Uncle Billy and their two boys. Suddenly we
had an overflowing house. The Templeys were able to save
the money they would have spent on rent and bills to help
pay for the house that they were having built in Sandhurst
Avenue. Dear Annie was leaving us and getting married, so
her room would be available.

Mother and Auntie Lottie, her younger sister by only eighteen
months, were close like Micie and me. They would be able to
run the house and look after four small children and a baby
between them, and Mother would save money by not having a
maid. Sleeping accommodation was limited with the influx of
four extra bodies. So Micie and I and the two Templey boys
slept four to a bed – not lengthways but from side to side like
sardines in a tin – until we were separated for order's sake.

Auntie Lottie was even-tempered and easy to get along with. Quick to see the funny side of things, she had a laugh that was almost a giggle. She and Uncle Billy were to become great favourites of ours. We learnt later that Uncle Billy could be thin-skinned. His temper could flare up quickly but it didn't last long. It was usually directed at his two boys, our cousins John and Colin. The rest of the time he was calm and patient. He was very interesting to talk to, he knew a lot about all manner of subjects; he was a clever man. Had he not been born into a poor family and therefore unable to have a good education, he would have trained to be a doctor. That had been his ambition – as it had been mine – the first of my many ambitions. As it was, he was apprenticed to the large engineering firm of Ransomes, Sims & Jefferies on the wharf at Ipswich Docks. Uncle Billy climbed the ladder from the shopfloor to become part of the management.

The Docks are now a marina with hotels and boats, and they are home to the University Campus of Suffolk. This I know because an honorary doctorate was conferred on me – the easiest way, I find, to gain a degree.

One evening, not long after they came to stay, I was sent up to fetch our nighties and as usual, I threw them down the stairs to the hall below with its floor of polished wood and its square of Axminster carpet in the centre. Unfortunately, the nighties landed on the floorboards and I ran downstairs after them.

As I scooped them up I found I had scooped up a large tri-angular splinter as well, under the nail of my middle finger. It was Uncle Billy who tended to me. He soaked my finger in a cup of hot water and iodine for five minutes and then, using Mother's eyebrow tweezers, he drew it carefully, slowly, out of its lodging place. It didn't hurt one scrap and didn't become infected either. He told me then, a child who was five years old, that you must always soak a splinter so that the wood fibres cling together as they swell during the soaking and then it can be drawn out completely, not leaving little bits of wood behind. Thirty-five years later I used his expertise to remove a splinter from under the toenail of my youngest daughter, Naomi, when she accidentally hit her barefoot against the wooden heel of a shoe being worn by our happy, friendly Norwegian au pair. Naomi kicked up a fuss, not like me.

I wonder now at how obedient we were but Father had instructed us, often enough, 'Do as you are told' and 'Children should be seen and not heard'! That must be the answer – we were afraid.

John and Colin were not tamed so easily, being boys. Uncle was very strict with them. I think they suffered a few beatings on their bottoms. Colin could be a bit sly when he was little and would provoke John into retaliation and then he would cry out, 'John's hitting me!' Poor John would get the blame. Once, Father, having a slightly devious streak himself, became suspicious. Creeping up the stairs, he listened outside their bedroom door and overheard the whole scenario; Colin got the blame that time! So Father could be helpful sometimes.

The only time I ever remember him being kind to me was when I was alone in the single bed of Annie's old room. I was sharing with Micie; we'd been separated from the boys by now – there had been too much playing when we should have been sleeping. I was sitting up in bed and Father was there with a bottle of syrup of figs – a laxative. I must have had a stomach pain and been put to bed with a hot-water bottle. He put a spoonful of it in my mouth and I was promptly sick in his hand. Realising what was about to happen, he had saved the bedclothes from harm! I simply hated syrup of figs; even now the smell of it makes me feel ill although I love figs.

Father said, 'You don't have to take it ever again', and I was so grateful to him. Ever after, if Mother tried to dose me with it I would say, 'No, Daddy says I don't have to have it.' And I never did: Father's word was law.

Mostly, we children played happily together. We played families: John and Micie were husband and wife, and Colin and I were the other mister and missus. We seemed to make them friendly relationships; I have no recollection of married rows, but then Uncle and Auntie were happy with each other. Perhaps they were our ideal and we copied them. Rosebud was occasionally included as Micie's baby.

We loved the Templeys being with us; it was interesting to do different things. Micie and I dressed Colin in my blue-checked cotton dress once, to make him into a girl. He had a pretty face as a child with a mop of black curls. We thought it was very funny. We were always laughing except when, being boys, they teased us.

It would have been Colin, of course – he was the lively one who once chased us round the garden holding up an earwig. He'd discovered that we were terrified of earwigs – we thought they crawled into your ears.

That night I had a frightening nightmare. I dreamed that I was in bed, and it was crawling with earwigs. In my terror

I climbed on top of Micie to get away from them. Poor Micie started to cry. Mother came in, saw me on top of her and lifted her out, taking her to sleep with her – leaving me to sleep with the earwigs!

It's worrying how parents get the wrong end of the stick. I've done it with my own children unwittingly.

Mother owned a tiny Singer Junior car by this time. She'd take us all out in the afternoon, Auntie Lottie beside her with Rosebud on her lap, Micie and me on the back seat and the boys perched on the inner wheel arches – very uncomfortable – poor things.

One memorable day the car came to an unexplained halt in a quiet country lane. We all got out – quite thankfully, in the boys' case. Mother picked up a stick and unscrewed the petrol cap to see if there was enough petrol in the tank – which there was. That was the only reason that a car wouldn't work as far as she knew, so she was stymied.

Suddenly we heard the sound of a motorbike approaching from the opposite direction. Auntie and Mother took up their positions across the road in front of our little jalopy, with legs akimbo and arms outstretched.

The motorbike slowed down, and stopped just in time. The rider turned out to be one of Father's electricians! Serendipity! Up went the bonnet, a few adjustments were made to the carburettor or the points – then bonnet down, thanks given and we were sailing merrily along again.

On another occasion we landed in a ditch but we all managed to push the car out again – it was so light.

Then Mother had an accident. She was on the way to visit Father at work and had stopped at the traffic lights in Carr

Street opposite the famous White Horse Hotel. She put her arm out of the window to indicate that she was turning right into Northgate Street where Father's business was. Mother started to turn just as a female cyclist overtook her. She hit her back wheel, causing both girl and bike to fall. She visited the girl in hospital, who was luckily only bruised. Although the girl admitted it was her fault – she thought she could get past her – it upset Mother so much that she gave up her little car and with it our jaunts.

The Templeys' house was completed all too soon for us children and they went to live on the other side of the town, so we didn't get to see them very often after that. Although we missed Auntie's cheerfulness, Uncle's good humour and our happy times with John and Colin, I started school with Micie soon after they left and so we were quickly distracted from our loss.

What a timid little creature I was on my first day at school. I didn't even dare raise my hand in Class 7 at St John's when I wanted to go to the lavatory. At break we were given our small bottles of milk. The additional liquid contributed to my woe and I wet my chair seat.

Mrs Cocksedge asked what it was and I fibbed, 'I spilt my milk.'

'You didn't, you wet yourself, you naughty girl.'

I felt quite ashamed, but the trouble was the children's lavatories were in the boys' playground, and playtime was almost upon us. Soon the place would have been alive with boisterous boys when I came out of the lavatory, and how would I have got to the girls' playground?

I would have had to go back through the school building or dodge the wild antics of the herd of boys to reach the safety of the girls' playground. It's amazing how fast thoughts travel in just a few seconds when you find yourself in a desperate situation!

Those little lavatories, very low, were in cubicles in a row with definitely no flushes. Every so often they would flush simultaneously, regardless of any occupants. When a teacher visited the large one at the end of the row, she would use her chain. There was indeed a chain reaction! It could give you quite a shock if you were sitting on the loo at the time.

By the following year, in Class 6, I felt at ease. We learnt our ABC and started to read using that method, not phonetics. We chanted our times tables until they were ingrained and went on to do our sums.

As more of a playtime lesson we were taught to knit. I was happy knitting as I'd been doing it for three years, having learnt to do it while at Miss Tracey's kindergarten.

I wonder what the boys were doing as they sat in rows at their desks? They couldn't have wanted to knit dolls' bonnets. We were very well behaved – no rowdy behaviour or unseemly noise in our school. The boys could let off steam in their own playground, separate from the girls' playground at the front, which had a more sedate atmosphere.

We girls were making a long strip of garter stitch, which our teacher Miss Price was going to turn into dolls' bonnets. Miss Price took our strips of knitting home with her – there must have been at least fifteen of them, if not more, according to the different proportion of boys and girls in our class of thirty pupils. She folded them in half lengthwise and sewed the edges together on one side, gathering them up, turned back the unsewn side – for decorative purposes – and attached ribbons to the bottom of that fold. Pauline Russell, who Micie and I would call for at her house and take with us to school, was very poor at the craft, producing very loose, loopy stitches. In fact, Pauline's pitiable attempt at a bonnet was so droopy that Miss Price added a lining of blue material to it. I thought that was very unfair. To be rewarded for poor work! I was always very keen on justice. This was before I learnt that life was unfair and you become an adult only when you accept that. Virtue is its own reward! I find I constantly have to remind myself of that. Pauline was to become an indefatigable knitter, making intricate fairisle patterned jerseys. She out-knitted me.

On the next step up in our progress through infant school we found ourselves in a classroom that seemed to be made of what we would have called 'blackboards'. They were, in all honesty, more grey-looking than anything else, but these served as our exercise books in Class 5. Each pupil stood at their personal board and wrote their answers to questions or did their sums on it. We added up, took away, multiplied and divided.

Once, during a 'question time', I was asked to write down what my father did for a living: I had no idea. Turning to Vera Starnes on my right – I remember her clearly because we had the same birthday – I asked her in a whisper, 'What are you going to put?' 'A businessman.' So, I wrote 'A business-man'. It was actually true, but how was I to know? As far as I was concerned, he went out in the morning, he came home in the evening and he provided the money. What more did I need to know? And why did Miss Downing want to know? It was nothing to do with her. How impertinent!

I was very unhappy at school in the autumn term of 1934. Had Micie lived, I would have had her as a support, as we would have both been in Class 3 together. Using sarcasm and with no acknowledgement of the fact that I had jumped Class 4 and a whole year's work, our teacher Miss Ray would constantly criticise me: 'Look at you – always in the middle. Never at the top, never at the bottom.' Mother must have noticed that I was miserable. I wouldn't have said anything. I had become very quiet after Micie's death, but I must have seemed unusually so, which prompted Mother to ask if there was anything the matter.

'Miss Ray is bullying me,' I said.

Unbeknown to me, Mother went to see the headmistress, Miss Mills, and said, 'You know that the child has lost her sister and Miss Ray's treatment of her is adding to her unhappiness.'

I did notice that Miss Ray began to treat me better. And I do remember, later on, going home and saying, 'Miss Ray was very nice to me today.'

I was talking of this, not long ago, to Rosemary and she asked me if I had known that Miss Ray had been suffering from cancer at the time Rosebud must have overheard Mother telling Grandma. I hadn't known.

Chapter Six

We hadn't stayed long at the house in Grove Lane, but moved to 33 St John's Road. Apart from Warwick Road, we were happiest there. Mother was pleased with the garden. It was pretty and quite wide as the house was double-fronted, which Mother liked. Meaning that the front door was in the middle and there were bay windows on either side for the dining room and the drawing room. The drawing room also had French doors which led into the garden. The move meant I was nearer to Pauline Russell and Pam, her elder sister by nine years.

Pam would take us to the pictures at the Odeon, the Gaumont or the Regent, the three big cinemas in Ipswich. She'd buy us ice-cream in special ice-cream cups – it was always green mint. Pauline acted as if it were the Holy Grail. She had this knack of making even the simplest things seem special – what a gift. But the outing I remember most vividly is going with them to their Auntie Maud's beach hut at the Brackenbury Fort end of Felixstowe. It was at night and the hunter's moon was full, with the tide at its lowest, revealing rocks that at other times we never saw. We walked far out on them looking at the sea urchins, with the great moon in the sky; it seemed a very romantic and exciting thing to do.

Pauline was to become my closest companion. We played dressing-up games in the attic of her house in Spring Road. Pam's dance dresses that she'd discarded were kept there in a box-trunk with a rounded lid. We'd put these on our unformed figures and re-enact scenes from the films we'd seen, taking it in turns to be the man. Later we would go to church together, the youth club and the cinema.

The attic room was also the converted bathroom, in that a large claw-footed bath stood out from the wall at one end with a brass geyser attached to the wall beside it. The geyser was the forerunner of the Ascot water heater. They were considered quite dangerous objects, and the fear was that they would explode upon ignition.

We were never allowed in our bathroom when father undertook the operation – the pilot flame was lit, then came the anxious moment of waiting to see if all the jets would safely roar into high yellow and blue flames. Relief – and hot water – and we were allowed in!

Father had his aviary again, now at the top of the garden above the rockery that bordered the lawn and there was a chicken shed, which Rosebud and I used as our playhouse. Lupins grew in the garden – I have tried to grow them many times since, without success.

We had two pianos at Number 33, after Father came home one day with a baby grand. The upright piano was relegated to the dining room and the baby grand took pride of place in the drawing room. Rosebud was encouraged to stand on the piano stool and sing, while Mother played. At the age of five, Rosebud had a lovely singing voice. I decided to get up on the stool one day and was promptly told, 'Get down, you can't sing.' It's a wonder I survived with any confidence at all, but then again I didn't.

Looking back, I recall that Father was always bringing things home. In Warwick Road there was our dear little Yorkshire terrier Smokey, who we didn't have for long, the used paints and the chocolate rabbit, and the lights that adorned the Christmas tree. He might have bought Chip as well.

At Number 33, first to arrive was a small Pekingese, reddish in colour. Unfortunately, Rosebud and I had bare feet when he met us and he tried to bite our toes – we leapt on to the sofa and so Father returned him to wherever he came from.

A stuffed fox in a glass case came next, which was placed on a sideboard facing the upstairs lavatory door. This lavatory door was next to the bathroom door at the end of a space about the size of a box room but which was not usable as a bedroom since there was no other access to the said loo and bath for the other three bedrooms.

Every time you needed the loo, you had to go from the landing through this 6 by 8-foot space and past the fox with his beady eyes. I always imagined he was looking at me ready to pounce and I'd pluck up the courage to run past as fast as I could before he could spring, and shut myself into the loo.

Thank goodness, when we next had to move Father must have needed money and he was sold off.

The baby grand piano was one of the last objects to appear on the doorstep and that didn't stay long either, being handed over to Auntie Marie in lieu of a wedding gift when, that summer of 1935, Uncle Eric and Auntie Marie were married.

Auntie Marie and Uncle Eric stayed at the Sheiling Hotel in Yarmouth on their honeymoon. They spent their first night sitting – Auntie in her new satin nightdress, part of her trousseau, Uncle in his pyjamas – on either side of the bed, too shy and embarrassed to get into bed together after an eight-year engagement, I learnt much later. Auntie was still unsullied after her 'first night'. They'd had a few upsets during their engagement: Auntie told us they'd quarrelled one night and she took her opal engagement ring off and threw it away in the street. Uncle went to look for it in the daylight and, luckily, found it! This kind of thing was probably caused by frustration, and yet when the opportunity arose for satisfaction, they – in their virgin state – hadn't the faintest notion of what was expected of them or didn't dare attempt it.

When she was a small girl Marie told her mother – my grandma – that they must keep pigs in a nearby house as she'd seen one's tail through the front door. She had no idea that there was a man behind it!

At our last house, just up and across St John's Road at 154, another Yorkshire terrier came home with Father and he was called Joey. We loved him very much and he was with us until he died. The next to arrive was a golden retriever, Prince, who was very comforting to lie down by and snuggle into you when you were miserable. Rosebud loved dogs and still does. She's got one now named after her doll, Trixie. Then a cat came, and a Turkish carpet and a smaller mahogany piano. We even had some new furniture from a shop! A salmon-coloured, damask-covered Thirties-style suite with long seats and short backs, and some new bedroom furniture (we still shared a bedroom Rosebud and I) – it too was in Thirties style, with a low dressing-table and a huge looking-glass where I used to sit at six o'clock on a Monday morning to do the homework I hadn't done during the weekend (rather as I'm doing now, but seated at the dining table at 2.30 a.m., going to bed late, when I should have got up early instead).

We went to Hunstanton for our summer holiday in 1935. In the car on the way there, we had a frightening experience. Reaching a junction of five roads with no roundabout, Father, exiting the junction at half-past twelve to take the fourth exit at ten-past one, was approached from the left by a car going at speed from twenty to one towards the fifth exit, or quarter past one.

Father managed to steer the car into our exit, narrowly avoiding a collision, but we ended up on the wrong side of the road. The sudden braking caused me to bite my lip and Rosebud to fall off her seat and bump her bottom – which made her laugh as she thought it was a joke. Mother and Father were a bit bruised and shaken.

The incident drew them closer together for a brief time. I can picture them walking along the beach at Hunstanton, in front of Rosebud and me – Father with his arm round Mother's waist. It was so unusual that it has stayed with me.

Our parents weren't usually affectionate. As Auntie Lottie said, her affectionate side was killed by her relationship with father. Sometimes when Father used to try to give her a peck on the cheek she'd say 'Oh no, Harry' and turn away with distaste. We were very affectionate with our maternal grandparents, though, and with our auntie Marie and uncle Eric – we got a lot of affection from them.

That Hunstanton holiday was the only occasion Father took us shrimping. Both Rosebud and I loathed it. It was bitterly cold that year on the north Norfolk coast and there we were, knee-deep in icy water, pushing these shrimping nets attached to long heavy poles along the sea bottom and bringing out strange brown things that turned pink when the landlady boiled them for us. I had never seen a brown shrimp, but they tasted very nice. Rosebud and I did not enjoy that holiday; we had much preferred Yarmouth.

In the months following that holiday, we began to wonder why Mother's stomach was getting so big. An old rocking chair with long black runners appeared and Mother would sit in the morning room, rocking. We asked her why her stomach was so big and she said it was wind. We didn't question this. I was eight years old and I hadn't started at the High School yet, where I would learn that our reproductive processes were the same as a rabbit's!

Rosebud and I woke up on the morning of 23 April 1936 to be told that we had a new baby sister. We were rather taken aback. Mother had given birth to Lois during the night in the bedroom next to ours and we hadn't heard a sound. We thought the stork had brought her. She was in Mother's bedroom in a frilled cot that we had never seen before. A rather beautiful baby, she weighed ten pounds; the biggest of Mother's babies, a consolation for the child she'd lost.

Nurse Tripp was in attendance for a month, looking after mother and baby, giving Mother delicate meals of calf's-foot jelly, boiled eggs and grapes, as befitted an invalid who'd gone through the strenuous process of giving birth. Mother was kept in bed for a fortnight, followed by another fortnight of being allowed up under Nurse Tripp's care, to complete her recovery. However, she was most upset with Nurse Tripp. After giving birth to her previous four children, she had had a bandage wound tightly round her stomach to flatten it. But by 1936 this had become an old-fashioned idea and instead exercise was 'all the rage'! But Mother was not a woman given to sporting activity. Lois was a big baby and her fifth child, and in later days she often blamed Nurse Tripp for not binding her up like an Egyptian mummy and leaving her with what she called a 'high stomach'.

Initially Rosebud and I were not very pleased with this baby. Nobody took any notice of us when they came to visit; they cooed over the baby. I think it affected Rosebud more than me. She was jealous because it was she who had been the adored youngest child. She says she remembers walking beside this elegant pram with the new baby all dressed up in a white organza bonnet and beautiful new clothes, while she was wearing her old hand-me-down navy school blazer. For the first time, she felt very dowdy and unloved.

I dropped the new baby, Lois, on her head once. Mother had sent me outside to bring her indoors. Rosebud was with me. I took the brake off her fashionable pram, which had huge wheels and a shallow body, and it tipped up and Lois slid out backwards. I hastily scooped her up and took her inside. She seemed to survive quite well, and Mother wasn't to know!

We certainly weren't considered capable of feeding or changing her, so our mothering instincts weren't brought into play. We simply weren't included. My own two eldest girls, Louise and Sophie, at the ages of seven and five dealt expertly with changing their youngest sister Naomi's terry-towelling nappies, fastening them with big safety-pins; and they bottle-fed both her and their cousin Sarah, who were born a month apart.

Rosebud, who we called 'Buddy' from this point on, says that she felt overshadowed by my cleverness, which added to her woes. At school, Buddy was always being told, 'Oh, your sister would have got more marks than that.' Or 'Oh, take that smug look off your face; your sister would have done better than that.' This seemed to happen even if she got something like 17 out of 20 in a spelling test.

Although I had struggled in Class 3, I did catch up with my work, and by the time I was nine and in Class 2 I was always first or second in the class, alternating with a boy called Kenneth Pallant who was a year older.

Aged nine, in Number 154, I was living closer to School. One or two hundred yards down the hill were Pat Beales and her brother David. Pat was my age and in Class 2 with me, and Rosebud had started school at the same time as David had. Pat's father was a lay-preacher in his spare time. What his occupation was I didn't ask and never knew. They lived in a big house and you walked up a sloping path as it was set on higher ground, dotted with trees, than the houses on either side.

Pat was a bit mischievous, perhaps because her father set her high moral standards and she needed to break out from them occasionally. Whatever the reason, one day when we were in Austin's sweet shop on the corner of Spring Road she encouraged me to steal a toffee. I, being fearful of breaking the law and knowing it was wrong to steal, did so very reluctantly. I was following my leader but terrified that Mr Austin would have been looking through his little spy-window in his stock room, and come bursting through and clap me in irons.

Despite my lucky escape, that was the only sweet I ever stole from Mr Austin.

I went with Pat, David and Mr Beales to a country church where the preacher was an evangelist. It was Easter and he was talking of the crucifixion of Jesus. It made a great impression on me; I was very moved by it, feeling a powerful sense of pity for Jesus.

This must have been the beginning of what developed into a strong faith, a belief in Jesus being the mediator between us and that power of creative love which formed the universe, with us as part of it.

This did not come easily. In my twenties I examined it, read numerous books of different approaches to the question of its truth. Much shaken by some, I've continued to hold on to my faith.

Driving further down our road just around the corner at the bottom of Spring Road was Pauline's house. That was the family that I was drawn into by Mrs Russell and Pauline's elder sister Pamela. People didn't show any open sympathy. I only learned years later what their feelings had been.

Mrs Russell told me 'I used to feel sorry for you standing alone on the doorstep'. I just remember her smiling.

So I was part of them. Often, on our way to school we were joined by Eric Lockwood. He had lived a few doors away from our Warwick Road house when I would continue to Granny's house with him sometimes, we would walk to the bus stop where we waited for the trolley. He was a bit older than us but now we were all in the same class (as Pauline, like me, had jumped a year) and we became very friendly. I thought of him later as my boyfriend in the sense of a boy friend, but I would use his surname when I was acting Lady Lockwood with Rosebud three years later.

One day when I was going on to Granny's house without Eric, there was a man painting some hoardings. He had reached the far end. I couldn't resist touching the paint at my end with the tip of my forefinger to see if it was dry. He shouted at me and, very scared for the next week, I walked the long way from school, down Woodbridge Road and in a pincer movement came upon Granny's house from the opposite direction. This to make sure that the coast was clear.

I still have this impulse to touch things, I'll run my hand over a sculpture. But I think you're supposed to feel the texture of material, wood, skin.

When I was fifteen and Eric was sixteen I met him again. I can only remember us walking from the cemetery towards Woodbridge Road and what dress I wore. It was pale lemon, patterned all over by flowers, nicely fitted and fastened with buttons down the front. I have a sense that we were going for a walk together and the memory has stayed with me because we hadn't a word to say to each other. We walked in silence, he beside me on the outside of the pavement. Gone was the easy relationship of childhood. That was the last time I saw him, that good-looking dark-haired boy.

If Micie had been there to say 'Don't June, it's dangerous!' I might not have held on to the iron palings with their sharp spikes in the playground and swung my right leg backwards and forwards until on one high backward swing my foot came down and was speared on one of the sharp spikes. I lifted it off and told no one, although there was blood staining my white ankle socks. Back in the classroom, 'Please Miss, June Brown's foot is bleeding,' one of the girls piped up. Off to the headmistress I was taken, to her small glass-walled office I suppose. I'd only seen this room on my way through the school entrance but that day I remember stuffing my hankie into my mouth to stop myself from making a noise, as she poured neat iodine in the hole. Luckily the spike had gone in beside my toe joint. She bandaged it up and I went back into the classroom and after school would have walked home or to Grandma's house.

I'm glad it was then and not now, as I'd be doing the cleaning and bandaging myself or be taken to hospital to have a tetanus injection.

I was the only one at St John's School to win a scholarship to the Ipswich High School the next year, one of the twenty-five schools in the Girls' Public Day School Trust. These were highly academic schools where most of the girls were expected to go on to Oxford or Cambridge. The word

'Public' has now been dropped – perhaps that sounds too elitist for these times!

My friend Pauline was going to the Jesus and Mary Convent School, so I would be starting this new school on my own. On the first day of the autumn term 1937, I felt very apprehensive as I took the trolleybus into town and then walked up the long hill that was Westerfield Road towards the school. That apprehension was justified when I found that I was to be put into the Lower Third with the other ten-year-olds. I had gained a scholarship a year in advance but far from being an achievement, it was of no relevance. At the High School I would be in the class appropriate for my age.

I was now to mark time, repeating the work I had done at St John's. To make matters worse I found that winning a scholarship carried a stigma. The three scholarship girls, all strangers to each other, were handed out used textbooks in front of the fee-paying girls who had their new books in their satchels. I felt rather inferior. I felt even more of an outcast when, in answer to the question 'Who has brought their lunch?' I raised my hand and held up my apple. I understood lunch to be the mid-morning break, not a cold meal at midday. I didn't feel that I'd got off to a very good start.

Fortunately, walking up the hill a day or so later, I was joined by a small girl with dark-brown bobbed hair, a fringe, eyes browner and cheeks rosier than mine, who seemed immediately familiar. Kathleen Flory lived outside the town with her father, who was the headmaster of a village school. Although her mother had died, Kathleen was a bright, cheerful girl who was imaginative and funny. We became friends. I was particularly impressed when she told me that her father's foot had been blown off in the Great War – still in its boot! She once found a book hidden under a sofa cushion which was quite 'risqué'. She would memorise passages and recite them to me as we walked together to school. I vividly recall 'Her breasts hung like bunches of grapes.' It didn't strike me as an odd description at the time – it does now.

I was happy again. I had my friend Kathleen at school and Pauline to be with at the weekends. My misery slipped away. Micie became more of a distant memory – she was where we went with flowers for her grave on Sunday afternoons. Though it occurs to me while writing this that Kathleen was very like Micie – so perhaps she wasn't such a distant memory.

I started to enjoy my time at the High School. We were taught to play tennis, and netball: I was good in defence in netball but no use at attack – I couldn't get the ball in the net. We also learnt to swim that first term with a strange inflated sausage-like object strapped to our backs, which kept us afloat with the help of a cork board to hold on to, while our legs propelled us along.

I grew to love swimming and gained the Bronze Medallion for Life-Saving and Bar. The Bar was for taking the exam twice. Unfortunately, I didn't progress to the Silver Medal because I wasn't able to dive – my knees would bend backwards and so my legs wouldn't stay straight. It could have been a legacy from my accident with the bicycle when I was five.

I can't believe that three years earlier Rosebud and I had slipped out of that little lodging house in Yarmouth without telling my mother we were going down to the sea. We couldn't swim! If she had known, she would have stopped us, or found two little heaps of clothes on the sand and no children!

Naturally, the lessons that year had been easy for me and I passed the four end-of-year exams with Honours and received a prize – a token to exchange for a book of my choice at the Ancient House in the Buttermarket in the town.

The Ancient House still stands with its priest hole in the attic – a relic from the time of the Reformation when Catholic priests had to have a secret hiding-place in case the house was searched. I exchanged my token for *Out with Romany* by G. Bramwell Evans. His *Out with Romany* programmes were broadcast on the BBC *Children's Hour*, and although performed in the studio the impression given was of 'Romany' and his friends going for countryside walks and discussing the plants and animals they came across.

Somewhere amongst my hundreds of books is *Out with Romany*, with its gold stamp of Minerva the goddess of wisdom on the cover and the school motto underneath, 'Before Honour Is Humility'. Perhaps that's what I was supposed to understand when I was put back a year! I came across the sequel, *Out with Romany Again*, at a church jumble sale long ago and bought it for a shilling – 5p!

I found solace in books, losing myself in them from the moment I could read at the age of seven when Micie died and my childhood lost its simplicity. Whenever I was on my own I would read. 'Where's June?' I'd hear my mother say. I'd be behind the sofa in the bay window lying on my front with my nose immersed in a book. I read anything I found, from the stories of Enid Blyton to *The Blue Lagoon*. My auntie Marie had the complete works of Dickens, which I'd finished by the time I was ten. We read *Grimm's Fairy Tales*, Hans Andersen, Edgar Wallace, Thackeray's *The Rose and the Ring*, and Charles Kingsley's *The Water Babies* was one of my favourites, which I realised later was an adult fairy tale about the fickleness of love when based on possessions.

I must cull my numerous books – when I can bring myself to do it. I have dozens of ancient Penguin paperbacks with yellowing pages which will never be opened again. Occasionally, when I'm feeling generous, I'll give one of my books away, but they are precious to me. I've read and reread most of them many times. They were sorted into appropriate sections once but soon got out of order – non-fiction, fiction, politics – general, not particular – spiritual matters, health, psychology, healing, poetry, plays and – an enduring favourite – detective novels to take me away from my own existence; an escape.

During our time at Number 33 St John's Road things weren't too happy. Father had gone bankrupt – through no fault of his own.

Before we were born, Father had been a produce buyer in Malaysia and had amassed half a million pounds. He invested this in German bank accounts, in 1912 and 1913 but due to the devaluation of the German currency at the end of the First World War, its value was reduced to £20,000. It was still a considerable sum in the early 1920s, though, and he managed to buy a house in Rayleigh, Essex, with custom-made pieces from Heal's – some of which still exist, spread around the family. Now, however, in the years building up to the Second World War, people weren't spending money and Father's electrical company began to suffer.

We had the bailiffs in for several days. They had lunch with us, Mother cooked for them. We all sat round the dining-room table which we didn't normally use in the day, and it was really rather strange. We treated them as honoured guests, even though we were terrified that they were going to remove all the furniture and leave the house bare. This had happened to my Great-uncle Harry who went bankrupt at the same time and for the same reason. The whole contents of their house were taken save for one double bed in which they had put their youngest daughter Pamela under strict instructions to feign illness. Apparently, in a case of bankruptcy, you couldn't turf a sick person out of their bed!

In the end, the bailiffs went away empty-handed as it transpired that everything was in our mother's name. Father was always handing Mother papers to sign, the subject of which she was ignorant. It worried her a great deal over the years, but in this instance her signature saved the rather expensive furniture, the legacy from Father's profitable years.

Due to our reduced circumstances we had to leave our nice house and garden to move further up St John's Road, to Number 154, where the rates were cheaper. It wasn't difficult to find houses to rent but Mother didn't like the new one. She missed her double-fronted house. She often exclaimed, 'I hate this elongated house!'

Mother had given up work upon marriage, but she had to go back after Father's bankruptcy. She worked in a millinery shop and sold hats. It was at this time that we had to do quite a lot of the housework, especially on Saturdays – we used to make the beds, wash up and light the boiler and keep it 'in'. I mean, can you imagine? I was about ten or eleven. You're not allowed to do it now, really, are you? Children wouldn't be thought capable these days.

I remember on one occasion when the boiler had gone out for the second time. I desperately needed some help to get it started again, Rosebud was playing the piano in the drawing room and I came in with the tongs in my hand.

I called to her 'Rosebud, quick, quick, get me some coal, the boiler's going out again!'

She didn't answer me and eventually came in very slowly and stood in the doorway looking so unconcerned that I suddenly got cross and threw my tongs at her. They hit her on the hand. The hands she played the piano with . . .

Well, it didn't bear thinking about.

Rosebud didn't say anything to Mother, though. We were always very good in that way; we didn't sneak on each other. We'd always protect each other. We wouldn't dream of 'getting someone else into trouble'. The other person might be frightened that you would – but you never did.

I didn't see my new friend Kathleen during the summer holiday of 1938 because she lived so far from me, but I was still great friends with Pauline, whom I saw every weekend. We did our usual things, going to the pictures in the afternoons, by ourselves now, as her older sister Pamela was working in the Inland Revenue office. We'd come home and act out the stories, still dressing up in Pam's evening dresses, low-backed with no sleeves, Thirties-style, in the attic.

Both of us had been given bikes by then so that we would be able to cycle to school the next term, saving the trolley fare and the trudge up the hill in the rain and snow. For me it was

exciting to be able to go further afield and explore the countryside – to go where I wanted to go, not be confined to the car
and go where my parents wanted to go. Freedom! Pauline's
family had no car but her bicycle was freedom enough for her.

One lovely afternoon we found ourselves on the road to
Felixstowe, the nearest seaside town, which was twelve miles
away. We were sailing along so easily, we thought it would be
fun to go all the way. We arrived, took off our ankle socks
and sandals, had a paddle at the water's edge and, having no
money with us to buy food or drink, set off on the return
journey. We were in for a nasty surprise!

We hadn't realised that the wind was behind us on the
way there and now it was against us on the way back – in
fact, a gale was blowing! Our poor little legs, not used to
more than one gym class and games once a week, were ped-
alling away like pistons but only eating up the yards rather
than the miles – a snail could have gone faster. Exhausted,
hardly able to draw breath and almost sobbing after at least
two hours of dreadful effort, we reached the outskirts of
Ipswich, where fortunately Pauline's Auntie Maud and Uncle
Harold had moved into their new bungalow on Bixley Road.
At the end of our endurance and worried about our parents'
reaction to our absence, we fell into Auntie Maud's arms for
comfort and reassurance and food! She had a telephone –
that was a relief! Not many private houses did then. Even
better, so did we – a relic left over from Father's attempts to
sell his bankrupt stock. Pauline and I could arrive home without having to give an explanation for our disappearance.

In the future we would make sure we knew which way the
wind was blowing. Useful in all sorts of ways.

Chapter Seven

In September 1938 I went happily back to school for the autumn term on my new bicycle, only to find that I had lost my friend. Kathleen had been taken away from the school and sent to one nearer her home. I'd had someone to share things with, talk to, laugh with and now she was no longer there; I was on my own.

Adding to my feelings of isolation, I found the work in the Upper Third difficult. In my year of marking time in the Lower Third, I had lost sight of the way to work. Learning had been so easy for me all the years before but suddenly it had become hard. Latin, algebra, geometry, physics and chemistry were added to the curriculum – I was over-whelmed. I struggled through that year with the work and made attempted forays into friendships, but none of them were fruitful. I wasn't used to trying to make friends;

with Kathleen, it just happened. I'd felt so at home with her.

I was invited to tea once by Mary Goodchild. Her name did not belie her – she was a very nice child. I mistook the invitation for a special occasion, so I put on my beautiful dress of gold shantung silk with a frilled Peter Pan collar and puff sleeves, tied at the waist with a brown velvet ribbon, and arrived at her home to find her wearing an ordinary cotton dress, ready to play in the garden. All I remember of that visit was feeling out of place and the two of us trying to make scent out of rose petals. We boiled the petals, which resulted in the final product smelling like cabbage water. She didn't ask me there again.

When Daphne Smith asked me to tea, I made sure I followed the correct dress code. I've no memory of what we did or said, but I can see us in her garden. We were both quiet children and needed a catalyst of another person to liven us up. Daphne's face was framed with small tight curls. We all longed for curly hair. Curls were the acme of beauty. They separated the pretty from the plain.

Mother had tried to give Rosebud and me ringlets when we were younger – 'hobnedobs' we called them – but she soon gave up her attempts. Rosebud had naturally wavy hair so her ringlets worked. However, I was left with ringlets that didn't last. Mother made one more attempt to satisfy my vanity by letting me have a permanent wave – the strands of hair were wrapped in squares of paper, soaked in perming solution and then plugged into holders on wires from a hood-like object. I thought I'd be electrocuted. It was quite a worrying experience and the disappointing results were funny, sausage-like curls, dangling from the ends of my straight hair. Actually, it wasn't funny at all.

I would have liked to have curls all over my head like Daphne and I wished for her lovely voice too, which was a clear high soprano. We performed *The Pied Piper of Hamelin* that year and she sang the lame boy who was left behind, 'Left all alone against my will'. I can still hear her. Her son wrote to me many years later upon the occasion of her eightieth birthday, very near mine, and asked if I'd send her a greeting. I did, but not before phoning him to ask if his mother had tight curls and a lovely voice. He laughed and said, 'Yes, she did.'

I phoned her then and discovered he had given her a flying lesson as a birthday present. 'What a change was there,' to quote *Hamlet*.

Lorna Tuddenham was another girl who was friendly, but she lived on the outskirts of Ipswich. We were slightly in awe of Lorna's elder brother – he was the actor Peter Tuddenham. I saw him long after in a TV adaptation of *Akenfield*, an enchanting book about Suffolk life in time gone before. He was the only one with a true Suffolk accent, and the right song to it. It goes up and down, you see. Rosebud and I would drop into it if we were together on the train as it neared Ipswich Station:

'Yew doin' alroight, geal?'

'Cahn't grumble.'

'Where ya goin', all alone together?'

And if someone was staring at you: 'Ad yer penneth?'

'No, oi want an 'apeny change!' (Quick with the repartee!)

'Oi'da loiked t'av bin in *Akenfield* only that Peeta all neva arst me! Woi not? is wot oi say. You'da thought eed've 'ad the sense!'

Not a West Country burr to be heard!

This being my friendless year at school, I spent more time with Rosebud. We had adventures and made up games to amuse ourselves. The best adventure was a foray into the gardens of the houses connected to ours. The house next door happened to be 'To Let' and at the end of their garden was another empty house which we could see from our back bedroom window, and it had a shed. What had they left behind in those gardens and that shed?

Rosebud and I couldn't control our curiosity; we had to find out. We planned to get up very early and go to see what we could scavenge and therefore to avoid trouble we rigged up a booby trap. This was a strange contraption consisting of a pair of plimsolls tied together with a long piece of string, which in turn was attached with a drawing-pin to the top of the door frame next to our bed, and then the plimsolls were wedged between the top of the door and the frame. The idea was that when the door was opened, the plimsolls would fall on to one of our heads and wake us up. Whoever was going to open it so early in the morning would have discovered our secret plan. The only boobies would have been us.

We woke up early anyway, dismantled the trap before it fell on us as we opened the door, and crept silently out. We were off – and a very successful raid ensued: we returned with three chipped flower pots, some half-empty tins of paint, one dried-up paintbrush and, to cap it all, a very heavy wooden trolley on small metal wheels, all balanced on this and hauled along with its thick wire rope. We were exhausted by the time we'd hoisted it over the two garden walls. Never mind, Mother wasn't to know. It occurs to me that not only were we very inquisitive but also very deceitful.

Our theft of this latter object turned out to be a mistake. Some days later Rosebud, thinking only of Lois's enjoyment, hauled the trolley as fast as she could down the garden path with four-year-old Lois perched on top. Lois fell off, as opposed to out. She tipped from the trolley and cut her chin. This time Mother did know. Her reception of what had happened was very frosty. Lois had to have three stitches.

Rosebud and I played doctors, schoolteachers and 'ladies'. We were rather snobbish; only the best would do. We had high aspirations far above our station, and even of that of 'the Lamploughs'. Our 'ladies' had the surnames of boyfriends in our respective classes whom we chattered away with as we walked home from school. We were Lady Lockwood (Eric) and Lady Beales (David), and our dolls were either patients or pupils at our private school, of course. Lady Lockwood or Lady Beales took it in turns to be the doctor or the fraught mother pacing the floor, wringing her hands and exclaiming, 'Oh! my poor child! Oh, my poor child!'

We only had the one script between us; we weren't good at dialogue. The other lady treated the child according to its injury – a brain operation would constitute sticking together the two halves of the chosen doll's painted papier-mâché head with a long strip of sticking plaster. If an arm or leg had suffered an injury, sewing cloth would be stuffed in to the appropriate places.

The unnamed private school owned by said ladies required more work as they set the papers, answered the questions and marked them up high or low, and also doled out punishments by making the 'girls' stand in the corner for poor work. The girls in the class who had had operations often didn't perform very well; allowances were made for them. Their names were Marie Bell, Jean Mansfield (not the filmstar, who had not yet been born), Judy Perish (come to think of it, she should have succumbed to her operation – why didn't we think of that? We could have had a funeral!), Annette Shuckle and Lydia (I can't remember her second name – she was probably rather dull, insignificant or shy, and easily forgotten).

In the 1930s as children we had so much more freedom. When I was nine and my sister Rosebud was six the two of us used to go to my Uncle Eric and Auntie Marie's beach hut in Felixstowe during the summer holidays. Felixstowe was full of beach huts, nobody slept in them it wasn't allowed. My Uncle Eric had made theirs himself and very well made it was, he'd painted it cream. It was situated on a green with the huts positioned in a square.

Mother would give us each half-a-crown, which is the equivalent of twelve and a half pence and out of that we would pay four pence ha'penny for a return ticket on the steam train for a twelve-mile journey from Derby Road Station, ten minutes' walk from our house, which was on the line into Felixstowe.

Rosebud and I would walk to the station carrying our bathing costumes, towels, half-a-crown and Auntie's keys to the beach hut. No food, we bought our lunch and tea and paid for our amusements out of our half-a-crown.

So off we'd go to the seaside and on the way from Beach Station to Auntie's hut we would stop to buy rolls, 2 ounces of butter and tiny pots of jam for our afternoon tea. We'd unlock the beach hut, change into our bathing costumes, carefully lock the hut and while away the hours on the beach.

Neither of us could swim then, we just paddled and played in the sea and with the pebbles on the beach and wandered about amusing ourselves. We'd go to Butlins which was a small amusement park. The 'Scenic Railway' was too expensive for us but there was the Helter Skelter with a mat to slide down on and the Crazy House which had mirrors that made you look all different sizes and shapes. We had a hysterical time in there screaming with laughter at the way we looked and then we'd play the penny machines. How times have changed – my daughter won on the penny machines last summer . . . £6 worth of Tesco vouchers! They were 5p a play, that's a whole shilling.

Rosebud found these very addictive, she managed once to profit by one and sixpence. Unfortunately, her luck ran out and she lost all she had. So what was left of my half-a-crown had to be shared between us for the rest of the day. I was far too cautious, if I put one in and lost it that was the end of it for me.

At lunchtime we would go to the fried fish shop for two tuppenny pieces of fish and tuppence worth of chips between us.

We were forbidden to light the Primus stove, far too dangerous. So instead of making tea we'd buy small bottles of Tizer or Vimto. Vimto was our favourite one.

When it was time to go home we'd tidy up, make sure the hut was locked up properly and with soggy costumes and towels make our way to the station to get the train home.

Mothers weren't worried that their children would be abducted or assaulted and we never had any fear at being out on our own. We enjoyed our freedom and took it for granted.

Chapter Eight

During 1939 at the age of twelve I had become very aware of what was happening in the outside world – from reading the newspapers and seeing the newsreels at the cinema. Gas masks had been issued, public air-raid shelters were being built and I knew that the terrifying prospect of war was imminent.

Father, staying at home himself, sent us away to Yarmouth for the last week of August, aware that it could be our last holiday for some time; which indeed it was, as the east- and south-coast beaches would be mined by army sappers against the threat of German invasion. During our week at Yarmouth we had heard the sound of gunfire out at sea while we were sitting on the sands. Everyone fled the beach, it was a naval firing practice, but we weren't to know. When we reached the boarding house, the landlady was standing on a step-ladder pasting strips of brown paper criss-crossed over the glass panels of the front door. 'They're bombarding us, they're bombing us' she greeted us in a panic, 'We're being bombarded'.

On Friday 1 September 1939, there came the news that Germany had invaded Poland; Britain had a pact with the Poles that we would go to their aid if they were attacked. So with great apprehension we returned to Ipswich, on Saturday 2 September. As we left the coach station we saw a group of young men returning from a football match at Portman Road, spread out in a line across the road, with arms linked, happily singing, and seemingly unaware that they would soon be called up to fight in a war:

South of the border down Mexico Way –
That's where I met my love . . .
When she came out to play . . .
– The mission being told me
– That I mustn't stay
South of the border, down Mexico Way.

I'll never forget it.

Back in 1938 Germany had already annexed Austria and invaded Czechoslovakia, at which point our Prime Minister, Neville Chamberlain, had flown to Berlin to meet with Adolf Hitler, who assured him that Germany had no more territorial claims in Europe. They signed an agreement to that effect, and Chamberlain returned to London, waving a piece of white paper and reassuring the nation there would be 'peace in our time'. We believed that in 1938; we didn't believe it now.

The following morning, Sunday 3 September, the five of us sat around the wireless, waiting to hear an emergency announcement from our Prime Minister. At 11.15 a.m., it came: 'I have to tell you ... this country is at war with Germany.' Words we had hoped not to hear, but knew we would. I can feel the atmosphere in that room now. We just sat there in complete silence. Afterwards there was another broadcast instructing us to be prepared for raids to start immediately.

From this point until the end of the war, every home was to be blacked out and every street light switched off, in order to make it more difficult for the Germans to find their targets. Air-raid wardens would be patrolling the streets, ready to knock on the door of any house showing even a chink of light. As Father was no handyman, Uncle Billy came round that afternoon to help him knock together some wooden frames for the blackouts. Thick black paper was nailed on to the frames, which were secured at each window with wooden catches so that we could take them down until dusk.

That very evening the first air-raid siren sounded – wailing like a banshee. We were terrified. All of us fled to the safety of the cupboard under the stairs and shut the door on Father, who had to stand in the hall! There we were, squashed in, struggling to put on our gas masks for the first time, with the nasty smell of rubber in our noses and rude grunting noises escaping from the sides of our masks as we breathed out – rather like unladylike farts! Lois, aged three, horrified at the sight and sound of our pig-like snouts, refused to put hers on, much to Mother's consternation. The all-clear sounded. There had been no sound of aircraft, explosions or gunfire. It was a false alarm.

Father would become an air-raid warden and I, his designated messenger. As the air-raid posts weren't equipped with telephones yet, my job would be to run like the wind, dodging bombs and anti-aircraft fire, carrying information from one post to another – a human carrier pigeon! Fortunately, we experienced very few air-raids in Ipswich, so I wasn't called upon to perform this rather perilous task. I was, however, taught to use a stirrup pump, which qualified me for school fire-watching duty when I was in the sixth form.

My only taste of dodging bullets came when I was thirteen, waiting at the trolleybus stop halfway down St John's Road. I looked up the hill to see if a trolley was coming when, to my horror, I saw a German fighter bomber. It proceeded to machine-gun its way down the road. I shot up a nearby flight of steps and arrived at the door to the local cobbler's workshop. I didn't go inside for safety – I wasn't a customer! I simply flattened myself against the door and when the plane had disappeared, walked back down the steps and waited for the trolley bus.

The first nine months of the war were called the 'phoney war' as there wasn't much fighting, but at home we had a large map of Europe on the kitchen wall with little flags pinned on it, denoting the positions of the German, French and English armies.

Father brought home a stranger once, an engineer he worked with, I think, and he had a very strong cockney accent. He was looking at the map of Europe and explaining the naval positions to us all:

'The British fleet is daahn-yare and the French fleet is daahn-yare-yeer.'

I asked innocently, 'What's daahn-yeer?'

Rosebud kicked my shin and hissed through her teeth, 'Down here!'

To cover my embarrassment, I chanted, 'England the Land of the Free!' and Rosebud joined in.

Chapter Nine

Returning to school a fortnight later for the autumn term, three new girls had joined the form: Eva Nussbaum, Roma Poole and Dorothy (although we called her Peggy) Griffin.

Eva was living with her sponsors and guardians, a very strict elderly Christian couple, who were childless. They lived three miles outside the town, at Foxhall. Eva, a German Jewish girl, had arrived early in the summer on the Kindertransport, leaving behind her parents and her eleven-year-old brother Bo in Berlin. Her parents could only send one child to England which one should they choose? They sent Eva, reasoning that a girl would be more vulnerable to harm than a boy, while hoping that Eva might be able to find sponsors for her brother once she had arrived. Eva told me that she had tried over the summer to find sponsors for Bo, asking everyone she met to take him in. One woman said, 'I would if he were a girl.' Eva replied, 'But he plays like a girl.' Had I met Eva sooner, I feel sure that my mother would have taken him as we had a spare room, but since we were now at war Bo had lost his chance of life.

I was drawn to Eva, partly because she was Jewish. My grandma was Jewish and, through her, my mother. What would happen to them, if the Germans were to invade England? I was aware of how anxious Eva must have been. Even though she didn't show it, her family back in Germany must have been in her thoughts all the time.

Roma and Peggy were evacuees from the London bombing. Roma's parents rented a bungalow a short walk from me, in Marlborough Road. Roma and her mother lived there for the duration of the war and her father came to see them occasionally from Ilford to stay for the weekend. Roma was very attractive, and had a good singing voice and played the piano well. She had learnt to ride a bicycle before the war and had fair hair with natural blonde streaks. We became good friends.

Peggy and her parents had rented a house in Back Hamlet, next door to Alexandra Park. Peggy became one of my best friends. I liked going to her house because she was an only child, so her mother paid us a great deal of attention – and also because she had a dog. Peggy loved animals and she had a white Pomeranian who she looked after herself; she took her for a walk before she went to school, brushed her, combed her and fed her. The dog was entirely Peggy's responsibility. She was very self-assured, which was probably why I liked her. Peggy was also very good with a needle and thread, and made wonderful clothes for her dolls.

Despite my earlier mishap, Peggy Griffin and I cycled to Felixstowe once with her father. He organised the whole affair – and with the regimentation worthy of an army. We cycled for a certain number of miles, stopped for a set time to rest, then halfway there we had a glass of still lemonade in a small café – it had to be still, not fizzy, as fizzy wasn't good for you while you were cycling. Other than the lemonade at Trimley I don't remember much more, except the fact that we weren't out of breath or cycling in agony against the wind.

I hadn't even heard the term 'to break friends' until one of my small girls used it in the Seventies. When we made friends we stayed friends. There was only one particular girl in our form who was unpleasant –would make very spiteful remarks to deliberately hurt her target. I was the first on the receiving end, Eva the second and finally Peggy.

I arrived at school one morning to be told that I wasn't to speak to Peggy. I can't remember the reason for it, but she had been 'sent to Coventry'. I remember having a terrible time when this happened: suddenly, nobody was allowed to talk to her. I felt awful as she was my closest friend in school. I knew her well as a straightforward, honest girl; I was very fond of her, but I was too weak and cowardly to go against the crowd. Of course, I felt dreadful about it but I didn't have the moral courage to stand with her against the form.

I tried to correct this past mistake many years later when someone in *EastEnders* was 'sent to Coventry' by the rest of the cast. Nobody was speaking to him because of some dreadful newspaper article that had come out. Anyway, I was away for that particular week when it all happened, but before I went back I thought to myself, 'There's no way I am going to ignore him, he is my friend and I shall go to lunch with him, I shall speak to him and I shall be his companion.' I could still remember the guilt at how absolutely cowardly I'd been with Peggy, and I decided it didn't really matter if no one spoke to me either – I was not about to do the same thing again. People did still speak to me, and soon after they also spoke to him.

Peggy went on to marry a man called Alan who had a large family – she lived in Faversham where I met up with her not long ago. In the end I lost touch with most of my school-friends but when you meet people who were your childhood friends you just pick up where you left off. You have your childhood in common and your youth – there is an under-standing there that you don't share with friends you make when you are older. Your childhood friends know you as you were – before the baggage of life and age attached itself.

In the summer of 1940 we were expecting invasion, so Father rented a double cottage, standing on its own in the country about eight or ten miles from Ipswich, and we lived there for the whole of the summer holidays. In this strange old house we had to go through one bedroom to get to another (an experience I repeated many years later in the dressing rooms at The Aldwych).

The mattresses seemed rather hard – whether they were straw mattresses I don't know, but I know we had no elec-tricity; we had oil lamps instead. The water was pumped up from a well in the garden and the lavatory was outside. There was a greengage orchard and an old pond in the garden, which was lovely. There was also a spinet that we used to play and I can remember playing 'I can see the Lights of Home'. I think it was a song sung by Deanna Durbin, and was popular around that time. We found a trunk full of old-fashioned clothes neatly folded and Rosebud and I were having an amusing time trying them on until Mother came upstairs to see what all the merriment was about and made us refold them and put them neatly back as we had found them. An old lady must have owned the cottage and died, leaving the house with its relics of the past.

It really was a lovely cottage, and if I hadn't been thirteen and restless I'd have loved it. I was extremely bored being there during that whole lovely long summer because I wasn't with my friends. I remember I used to lie in the fields reading, feeling out of touch; if I hadn't liked reading I would have found it intolerable. We had a photograph taken of us all in the grounds which I simply didn't want taken, but Father insisted. I look very self-conscious in it. (Where is it I wonder?)

Then, in the autumn of that year, I was evacuated to Western Park, a suburb of Leicester, with two other girls. We stayed with a Mr and Mrs Miller. They had no children and so they'd offered to take three girl evacuees. We all slept in single beds in the same room. They were very nice, very pleasant people. At the same time, Mother, Rosebud and Lois were evacuated to Burstinghall quite a few miles away, and I would go over on the bus to see them about once a week. Auntie Lottie was there as well with her twin girls Jacqueline and Julie, born eight months before Lois.

I wasn't a small child, being sent off without my family, as many small children were – with their gas masks slung round their necks and a few possessions – it wasn't that much of a trauma for me as it was for them; it was quite an adventure, really. The two other evacuees were Barbara Robinson and Cynthia Bowell and we got on well together so I didn't miss Pauline or my family.

Barbara Robinson was a very nice girl indeed, one of a close family – there was just her brother, herself and her mother and father. When we returned home I stayed with them on the first night of our arrival as my Mother and sisters weren't arriving home till the next day. It was peaceful and friendly there. Barbara was quiet and studious, but she was picked on by a rather unpleasant girl who was the ringleader in the class. She used to chant a horrible rhyme: 'Barbara Ruby Robinson thinks herself a treat, long, skinny, banana legs and umbrella feet!'

On one occasion the Millers took us to the theatre to see a musical play called *The Maid of the Mountains,* but at the end of the first act the sirens went and we heard tremendous sounds of gunfire and bombs so Mr Miller decided that we'd better leave the theatre and walk home. We could see the fires of Coventry burning in the distance and hear the planes and the explosions, anti-aircraft fire, see the search-lights sweeping the sky and occasional sighting of a bomber caught in the beams.

I'm not ever as frightened if I can see what's going on; it's when I can't that I get extremely agitated. One day I'd been standing by the kitchen door when Auntie Marie came gallumping across the empty plot from her bungalow and the next one and said, 'Quick, quick, Junie, down into the shelter!', bringing her neighbour with her and we all had to rush down into the beach hut which Uncle Billy and Uncle Eric had removed from Felixstowe and sunk into the garden. I can't see that the hut would have been much protection – it was covered with several feet of earth but I think it would have caved in very easily. It was then that I was quite scared because I couldn't see what was going on. I'm just the same at the dentist – I need the dentist to tell me exactly what is going on and then I'm calm. It's the unknown that worries me.

When we left the theatre I don't remember there being any panic at all; the curtain came down and people very quietly left. The performance went on – performances did – but Mr and Mrs Miller decided that as they were responsible for protecting us we would be safer at home in the Anderson shelter behind the house.

I remember once being in their air-raid shelter and a soldiers billeted next door was caught relieving himself in the garden. He was made to feel very uncomfortable. No one said anything, but he knew that we knew and we knew that he knew we knew! Poor boy. These days we'd think nothing of it.

While we were with the Millers we had to go to lessons at the Wigston Grammar School in Leicester, where we had our classes with Miss Midgely, a lovely young teacher, our Latin mistress, but unfortunately she couldn't keep discipline very well, she was too new to teaching and rather gentle. When we were back in Ipswich again she was also our form mistress and some of the girls started to let off stink bombs in class. She was out of her depth with us and probably the most difficult classes to manage are those of 13–14 years old, feeling their feet. I got caught for letting one off once. I was persuaded to do it. I wasn't the ringleader. I was sent to stand outside the door in the hall, which was quite horrifying because it was near to the headmistress Miss Neal's office, and I was terrified that she would come along and ask me why I was standing outside; fortunately for me she didn't. I didn't do it again.

We were supposed to be having a hockey practice one afternoon but I didn't like it, panting up and down the hockey field I used to get quite exhausted. I was never much good at long-distance running; So, as *Pinocchio* was showing at the picture house in Leicester, I decided that I would go to see that instead and, by a stroke of bad luck as I left the cinema, I bumped straight into Miss Midgely. She instructed me 'Come and see me tomorrow.'

Being a girl who was clever at wriggling out of things the first thing I said to Miss Midgely the following morning was, 'I've got a toothache.' So she, with great relief, I think, forgot all about punishing me for playing truant from games and took me to the dentist instead. That was punishment enough because going to the dentist then with their slow drills and lack of anaesthetic injections wasn't a very pleasant experience. In fact, we dreaded it.

I was only evacuated for a few months, because once Coventry was bombed and they started bombing the Midlands we all came home.

Chapter Ten

After the upheaval of bankruptcy, my father had obtained work as a civilian in the Air Force at Wattisham Aerodrome, in the accounts office. He was going to be given a commission until they discovered that he was one year above the age limit, much to his disappointment. But he finally managed to secure a job at the local yeast factory later when the son of the owner was called up into the forces. Father took over from him as the accounts manager.

A young Belgian Ralph Latimer was sent to work in his office under him by the owner, Mr Van Perlstein. Father discovered that Ralph had escaped from Belgium together with his mother and half-sister via the Dunkirk beaches, and was separated from them, having left them behind in Tolworth, near Kingston-upon-Thames in Surrey. Ralph was just twenty-four and had still been a student, but because of the invasion of Belgium he was unable to complete his degree at the University of Antwerp. He was French-speaking but fluent in English with no accent. Father felt sorry for him as he was living in digs on his own away from his mother and half-sister, so having talked it over with Mother he invited him to come and live with us as there was the spare bedroom. This had to be cleared of the remainder of Father's squirrelled-away bankrupt stock and his .22 rifle, left over from the days of shooting when we lived at The Hollies in Creeting St Mary, where I was born and lived for a short time when I was a baby. Father had loved his four-acre pheasant shoot, but it might have been grouse, I wouldn't know.

Ralph was about 5 feet 9, and had dark wavy hair and hazel eyes. I thought he was rather good-looking but he wore glasses, which wasn't considered attractive for either sex then. 'Men never make passes at girls who wear glasses' was the old saying. It was seen as a kind of deformity.

He became like one of the family and we really enjoyed having him to stay with us; it livened up the house. It was as if we had an older brother! He did become like one. Ralph borrowed an old bike from Uncle Billy and he and Rosebud and I would go out for cycle rides as well as for walks on Rushmere Heath where you had to be aware of the golf balls flying as it was also a golf club. We'd take Joey our Yorkshire Terrier with us and keep an eye open in case he made off with a golf ball. We'd go to the pictures and walk home singing songs walking in step to the rhythm as we sang. We were constantly singing. Mother would play the piano while we all clustered round singing the songs of the day with

Ralph giving us solos of Italian songs and arias. He had a very musical, well-trained tenor voice so he was happy to have a second home where we sang and played the piano – some better than others, I must admit.

He wanted to help me with my French, but I was too shy and too self-conscious to let him. I was just fourteen and was still gauche. Nevertheless, my feelings gradually became those of a much older girl, and from affection towards him as for a brother, I began to feel love for him. I began to call him Raoul, which was how he was known by his family in Antwerp, and privately I was Juanita to him. This must have become obvious to my mother and father, if not my sisters. Nothing was said. They all loved Raoul and didn't expect either of us to cross the boundaries. It was an affection that deepened into love on both sides during the next few years, but had ended on his part by the time I was eighteen. It coloured the way I lived for several years then and later in a different way.

His was an unusual and complicated story and was the reason for him leaving our family six months or so later. I only know the outline. I never questioned him; I just listened, fascinated, happy to be his confidante. I was never told nor asked for, the details.

His mother, whom I knew as Lydia Latimer, seems to have left his father when she was very close to giving birth to Raoul. He was born midway across the Atlantic on a British liner, so that gave him dual nationality – Belgian and British. I know that Alfredo Livio who was Brazilian was the name of his father and Raoul was christened Angelo Luis Livio, so that was his legal name. I have a faint recollection of him telling me that he spoke Spanish and German, so he may have studied languages at university. Lydia's next husband was American, living in Cuba. They had a baby daughter, named after her mother Lydia, but whom I knew as Baby Latimer.

Raoul, as I shall speak of him, was called up into the British army because of his dual nationality and was drafted into the medical corps because of his poor eyesight. We wrote to each other constantly and he came home to us for his army leaves. At Christmas he came back bringing us his chocolate ration that he had saved. I should have thanked him effusively for this sacrifice but I'd been hoping for a pair of ice-skates – how ungrateful and childish of me. And there wasn't an ice-rink nearer than London – Sonja Menie was a film star ice-skater, maybe I was influenced by her. He gave me two books: *The Story of San Michele* by Axel Munthe and a copy of *The Rubaiyat of Omar Khayyam*, in which he wrote me an inscription in French. Axel Munthe was a Swedish doctor (born in 1857), and the book is not just about the house – San Michele – but is the story of his life among the rich and poor and the light of the sun he loved that destroyed his sight.

I made a trip to the house 'San Michele', on the island of Capri, when I was on holiday in Rome with Michael Cashman, a dear friend from his time in *EastEnders*, and Paul Cottingham, his lovely partner.

While in Rome we visited every church, square and fountain, the Vatican and the vast ruins of the Colosseum. Every night my ankles became enormous, swollen from all the walking from morning until, thankfully, dinnertime. After we'd eaten, the two of them would go out to play, and although they very kindly invited me to join them I'd retire to my bed to read and elevate my legs; the swelling took a week to subside!

One day we took a bus to Naples and crossed the bay by boat to Capri, visiting the Blue Grotto where the water really is blue, not grey like the 'blue' Danube. On landing, we took the bus up to Anacapri. After lunch I asked if the Villa San Michele was very far. 'Just down that road,' I was told. Michael and Paul took the funicular to the top of the island and I found my way to 'San Michele'. There was a group of American tourists inside who disappeared from the end of each room as I arrived in it. It was as if it was just me in the house that I'd known for so long in my imagination. I recognised it all.

When I was playing Nanny Slagg in *Gormenghast* a few years ago we were on location at Wimbledon Common and using a house nearby that seemed familiar. The caretaker was around and I remarked that it reminded me of Axel Munthe's house at Anacapri.

'This was his house in London,' he said.

The same book brought me to the attention of Christina Foyle of Foyles bookshop on Charing Cross Road in London. She'd seen an article that I'd written in a newspaper about about one's favourite book. I'd chosen *The Story of San Michele*. She wrote to me saying that she had given a luncheon for Axel Munthe many years ago, and had also offered a second one to George Bernard Shaw – the lunch to be a vegetarian one this time. He declined, saying he wouldn't be able to bear the sound of so many people crunching celery!

*

Just after an unhappy Christmas, Raoul came to collect me to take me to visit his mother and sister leaving me with them for a week. Raoul spent a few hours in London, first where he took me to Hampstead and we had tea at one of the old-fashioned 'tea-shoppes' that lined the hill to the Heath, quite different from when I lived there ten years later. We'd been first to one of the many French restaurants that had appeared in London with the influx of the Free French, Free Belgians and all the other nationalities who had escaped from the invaded countries.

The restaurant was typically French, I realise now, one long table that everyone sat at. It was in the vicinity of Piccadilly Circus possibly in Orange Street. Then we went to Tolworth. His mother and sister were very good to me. Lydia was dark-haired and 'Baby', typically American, blonde curls close to her head, blue eyes and short nose.

When I came home from the week in Tolworth, Mother, Rosebud and Lois were quiet; their faces looked strained. Father took me into the kitchen and told me, quite gently, that my beloved uncle Eric had been killed in the week that I had been away. On his motorbike on his way to work, an army lorry had skidded into the back of his bike and he'd been thrown over the handlebars and his neck had been broken – it had been very quick, he would not have known that it was happening.

I burst into tears, threw myself into Father's arms and then instantly recoiled from him. It had only been on Boxing Day that he had ordered Uncle to leave the house after the hideous row with Father. 'Come on, Marie, put your coat on' were the last words I'd heard him say, and now I'd never see him again. I know it wasn't Father's fault but I could not accept comfort from him. He must have felt very rejected.

Uncle had been taken back to the bungalow and laid on the bed in the spare room, the one I'd slept on when I spent weekends with them. I saw him there when he'd been put into his coffin on the day of the funeral and Father took me into the room. He said to touch him on the forehead so that I wouldn't fear death. It was a hard experience for a girl who was just fifteen.

Auntie told me that she had sat with him, talking to him during the three days before the funeral. She showed no signs of grief but for her set face, and her hair that started suddenly to go white very quickly. She cried only once, harsh, racking sobs, when the clergyman came to give her words of comfort. She was furious with him for causing her to break down. 'That stupid, stupid man.' I can hear her saying at his graveside to me. She stayed with us that night – at least I thought she did, but how could she have stayed in a house when so shortly before Uncle had been told to leave? No, she would have gone back to Grandma's to her old room that was hers before she was married. Shortly afterwards she went back to Kesgrave and sold the bungalow that Uncle had built for them.

I wrote to Raoul, tears dropping on to the paper. He wrote very sympathetically to me and told me that Rosebud had written to him as well and her letter had been full of Uncle – nothing else. Raoul was much loved by all of us, we all missed him when he had to leave us for the Army. He had made our home a happier place – no rows, no arguments any more, just singing and talking together and laughter; we'd drawn him in to us, he was one of us.

Just as I reached fifteen there was a nasty blow to my self-esteem. I started to get spots. Not one of my other friends did, I don't remember a single spot on Pauline, Peggy, Roma, Eva or Mary and I'm sure Daphne didn't suffer (and she had her curls).

One should never underestimate the effect of this on any young person. Always aware, showing the good side of the face (only one spot on the left), lowering the face, there's one on your chin! Trying to sit always to the left or right of the person you're with, according to which side of the face is the more presentable. Looking up sideways, to the left or right according to which side you needed to fix your eyes upon another person, usually of the opposite sex. This caused you to look as if you were flirting with them in a tarty way. Your personality is misrepresented, misinterpreted. Always self-conscious, your freedom to express yourself as you really are is limited. Consequently you have low self-esteem.

I rid myself of this affliction within a fortnight and regained my confidence when I was twenty-one having tried all the remedies under the sun.

You will say it would have happened naturally but it didn't look as if that would happen to me. Here's what I did. I stopped using my Max Factor Pan-Cake base and powder. My face looked as if it had crawled out from under a stone not having seen the light for six years. I cleaned the oily (greasy) parts of my face with a solution known as Innoxa 41. This will not be on the market now but it was pure alcohol, the surgical one not gin. I had the sense not to get it near my eyes.

I went on a diet – I cut out all carbohydrates, no bread, no potatoes, no sugar, no cakes, no sweets, nor chocolate. I loved chocolate. I fried nothing. Instead I poached bacon, egg and tomato in a saucepan of water. My meals were of meat or fish and vegetables only, plus a breakfast of All Bran with stewed prunes, moistened with prune juice and one or two pieces of Ryvita and a scraping of butter and Marmite – no jam, marmalade nor honey.

I must add that I only had spots occasionally but I did not have really bad acne. Nevertheless, I'm sure it would go some way towards helping that as well. The diet also got rid of my puppy fat. I came off it gradually and never had a spot or extra pounds of flesh again. I had six pregnancies and never had 'sugar in my water'.

You are free to follow my example, no charge required. P.S. Avoid the three 'Ps' – pasta, pizza and pitta bread and the 'Ss' for sugar and sweets. Add c for no cream, custard and cooking fat.

If I'd known about the benefits of this diet when I was fifteen, how differently I would have approached life. Going to Miss Olga Wilmot's dance on a Saturday night at the church hall that she hired for her students of ballroom dancing would have been a much happier event.

Pauline's Auntie Maud and Uncle Harold had lived opposite us, with a passion flower covering the front wall of the house. It was unusual at the time and was the first one I'd ever seen. Pauline and I regarded it with reverence because of the Passion of Christ. Pauline said it bore passion fruit. I passed it daily for years and never once did I see it. She was indulging in her habit of seeing everything as 'special', that is what I suspect. Although Pauline and I had attended different schools,

we still went to St Mary-le-Tower church together on Sundays
and to its weekly youth club, the Tower Adventurers, as well as
attending Olga Wilmot's Dancing School.

Willy went into the Air Force at eighteen at the same time
as I volunteered for the Wrens as he was six months older
than me, Pauline at 17½ was left without either of us and
promptly fell in love with an American as you will notice, I
couldn't go to their wedding as I was in London finishing my
last term at the Old Vic Theatre School, but I dashed to
Victoria Station to meet up with them and wish them well
on their way to their honeymoon in Torquay.

She went back to an 'old faithful' but perhaps he wasn't
entirely, when he was away in the R.A.F., who knows?
Whatever happened Willy and Pauline stayed together for
the rest of their lives. I couldn't go to Pauline's funeral, I was
working, but I saw dear jokey Bill off a year later, sadly. One
by one I'm losing all my oldest friends.

Pauline had managed to twist her ankle just in time for her
wedding, and hobbled up the aisle in a long white dress and
with the aid of a walking-stick. I can't remember what she wore
for her going-away outfit – she was probably in donkey-brown
and pale blue, which were the favoured colours at that time.

Most of our girlhood activities – the dance classes, the
church, the youth club and Olga's Saturday dance – were not
only recreational and spiritual but were fuelled by our newly
awakened interest in boys. There were the choir boys, not to
mention the Reverend Mr Reginald Babbington, the charis-
matic vicar of the church of St Mary-le-Tower, who was
married with four children but whom we secretly adored
from our pews. At one time we took to going to church twice

on Sundays! We were quite religious girls, but the presence of the opposite sex added another dimension. Some of the boys went to the youth club, and others from Ipswich Grammar School learnt to dance with Olga Wilmot.

These occasions were the only means of acceptable contact with boys, and they led to walks, stilted conversations and the odd kiss – that was as far as it went. Willy Walker was the easiest of all of them to talk to – he was always at Pauline's house and the three of us were great friends. He was cheerful and always joking. He'd flirt outrageously with me but Pauline treated this with lofty disdain – as she treated Bill – since she knew he adored her.

I went to their fiftieth wedding anniversary. Bill had tears in his eyes when he spoke of his good fortune in having married Pauline; putting his arms around me afterwards, he said, 'Junie, did I disgrace myself?' His emotions were a little fuelled by the champagne.

I suffered a blow that year when Pauline met Bill. Raoul's letters stopped with no explanation. In early August I wrote to him but no reply came. I wrote again asking him to meet me in the tube station at Piccadilly Circus, the only place I knew in London. In spite of getting no reply I travelled there and waited all day, coming home disconsolate. It was three years before I learnt why he was unable to be there. On Christmas Day I went downstairs to see if there was a letter lying on the mat by the front door as I had done every day in hope. There was an envelope with his writing on it. I couldn't wait to read but all I held in my hand was a Christmas card. One that you would send to a distant friend with no special message. 'Best wishes for Christmas, Raoul', is that what it said? My mind has shied away from it, I don't remember. I went and curled up in my father's big old armchair by the empty grate and I wept.

Chapter Eleven

Although my love for Raoul underlay the rest of my school-
ing, I sustained the years and behaved like an ordinary girl,
even a child at times. Roma, Peggy and I became a group of
friends joined by Yvonne Kenney and Eva when she could
get away from her chores for her sponsors in Foxhall. It was
a loose connection; we'd separate occasionally into twos and
threes.

The child in me climbed trees with Peggy and Yvonne.
We found a hollow oak in Humber Doucey Lane, hammered
large nails into the trunk for steps and then climbed to sit in
what we called 'Quincy Cottage' – shades of Enid Blyton,
coincidentally the most famous old-girl of the Ipswich High
School joined by me. I shouldn't write that in a book, not
someone like me who was taught not to be vain, conceited or
boastful. I must remember my school motto 'Before Honour

is Humility'. (Would take a nasty knock) with sardonic humour – I must remember to be true to my upbringing and not be vain, conceited nor boastful.

Sometime in that year Father came home with three American soldiers in tow, more men far from home. He must have met with them in town possibly when having a quiet drink on his way home. They would become constant week-end visitors. They were cooks, their names Johnny Cameron, Bernard Harvey and Tony, whose surname I forgot and who didn't visit very often. They would bring meat and provisions with them when they came for the weekend so we lived rather well on their gifts. We became their home from home and Johnny's wife, Helen, sent us dresses, mine shocking pink cotton with cap sleeves and a bold black embroidered motif on the top left of the bodice. It fitted beautifully.

Bernard was a bit sweet on Mother. It didn't bother me as I was sixteen and felt good that she had someone who admired her and helped her in the house and gave her a happy day in London once in a while. Father seemed at ease but Rosebud didn't like him at all – she thought he was sneaky but she was only fourteen and close to Mother.

There were lots of innocent times with the opposite sex – walking Joey on the heath with Johnnie Cameron one afternoon when he came over a bit amorous but I nipped that in the bud very quickly. He was missing his wife Helen. Peggy used to visit us at home quite a lot at this time as our Americans would bring a pleasant young soldier home with them and Peggy was, in the language of the day, 'quite smitten'.

I had met John Catchpole who had been training as a pilot in Canada, returning back with pairs of nylon stockings and

Ponds lipstick with which to tempt the girls, I presume. He was fair-haired and very presentable and all I remember us doing was having lunchtime drinks at the Crown and Anchor, a hotel in the town hall square. I would have sweet sherry and wonder why I felt a bit dizzy on the trolley home. One afternoon cycling down Northgate Street past my father's first lucrative business of Wood & Co I heard him call my name. Peggy who was with me, as we were on our way to her home, said, 'June, there's someone calling you.'

'Ride on' was my answer as I stared intently ahead. She did and so did I. What? Let him see my face devoid of my pan-cake make-up? Make-up was strictly forbidden at school, if I'd worn it I would have been expelled like the girl who was seen eating an ice-cream in Woolworths. A spot or two would have been in evidence at the time, there always was. I don't think I saw him again.

I had decided I wanted to be an osteopath at school, but I'd dropped two O levels that I found quite difficult, chemistry and physics. I was the sort of person who held a U-tube by both sides and exerted pressure with my other hand, then found to my surprise that it had cracked. So I wasn't awfully good at Physics. I liked chemistry, though – particularly the analysis, because I've always had quite an analytical mind. I was interested in finding out what the substance was using various tests ... anything else to do with chemistry eluded me, I mean I was hopeless.

I was very good at biology. I was fascinated by the work-ings and I loved dissection. I got honours for my Biology O level exam – actually they weren't O levels, we took the

Oxford School Certificate – I matriculated because I managed to get a credit in maths. This you had to achieve otherwise you were unable to sit the Higher School Certificate, the equivalent of the present day A-Level exam and I needed to do this to study Osteopathy. I don't know how I did that. I was extremely good at arithmetic and got a distinction for it but I didn't care for geometry. I just about managed to learn theorems, so got a good pass in geometry but only a pass in algebra.

I went up to the School of Osteopathy, which was quite brave at the age of sixteen during the war, and got the prospectus and information.

I told my father about it – how I wanted to be an osteopath, and that you had to train privately but his reply was, 'I'm not paying for you. You're a girl and you'll only get married.' Coming from a family of three girls where I had had no competition from boys at all, it was a tremendous shock to hear that. Although everybody thinks it wasn't until the Sixties that girls wanted a career, marriage and children. You could do it all in the early Forties – well, at our school you could because it was academic. You were expected to have a career which didn't exclude marriage.

It was a lovely school – we used to go outside for lessons sometimes when we were in the Lower Sixth, we'd take our light fold-up chairs out to the years-old well-tended lawn and sit in the shade of the ancient oak tree. It wasn't like having lessons at all. At break we'd sit on the big window, large enough for a single mattress to gossip, exchanging confidences, being ourselves and not schoolgirls. We were treated more like young women. I remember fire-watching with Mademoiselle Barbier, who was our French mistress – you stayed in school all through the night together. I think I slept in the sick-room. It did not concern me where Mme Barbier rested – it would raise eyebrows now, I suppose, but it didn't occur to us that anything untoward would happen. We were doing our fire watching duty waiting to put out incendiary bombs with our stirrup bombs.

It is a theory of mine that you shouldn't pile too much into children's minds. I think that gradually you absorb knowledge and when somebody mentions that subject you find you know what they mean. I remember when I was about ten or eleven, wheeling my bike up the hill from school, going home for lunch, and this boy stopped by me. He was about fourteen and he wheeled his bike beside mine and we were chatting away; I was a very unsuspicious girl, we were an innocent generation. So there we were, pushing our bikes up the hill and as we arrived at my house and I was about to wheel my bike into the front garden he asked me the question 'Would you like a fuck?' Although I'd never heard the expression before and was saying 'I don't know what you mean', I realised that I did.

So this is what I'm saying: when the situation occurs, you know because everything has built towards it – like a marriage going wrong or somebody having an affair, you are always aware of moments which, when you know the whole story, fit into place. And I think it's the same with knowledge, which is why I'm really against teaching children and young people things they don't really need to know. Because they are 'knowing', absorbing it anyway, and when the moment comes that they need that knowledge, it's there. Well that's just my theory, I'm not a teacher – and wouldn't be one in these days for all the tea in China.

I thought if I managed to do two years of Lower Fifth chemistry and Upper Fifth physics Father might change his mind. One minute I'd be in the Lower Sixth and then I'd be in the Lower Fifth and then into the Upper Fifth, then back to the Lower Fifth and back to the Upper Sixth, and it became impossible to join it all up. So I gave up trying to do three years' work in one, and that's why I went into the WRNS. I think the chemistry mistress also decided to forget it because I simply didn't hand in any homework. I had the most wonderful variety of excuses and, in the end, she stopped asking for it because she knew I was overwhelmed.

Biology I'd loved. I'd stay behind when school finished after a double period of biology, my eye glued to a microscope. As I've said, I was very good at dissection – one day, a poor rabbit was gassed with carbon monoxide in a large square biscuit tin by Miss George, then ditto a frog. You pinned the frog, spread out on a cork board under water, and he was quite delicate and finicky to deal with. Nowadays, people would scream in horror at the thought, but we were not sentimental about field animals. I'll be thought to be very hard, which I'm not, but that was the practical side of our work, tying in with the information and diagrams in our textbooks. If you conduct a post mortem you deal with *people's* bodies, which I wouldn't care for so much.

I started to study for an A level in biology when I was about forty, and thought I would perhaps train as a doctor. I was given a locust to dissect. Obviously, people don't care about locusts so it's all right to dissect them, but they're extremely difficult to work on because they have hard cases, carapaces. It was very difficult and uninteresting. Perhaps if I'd done my doctor's training I would have become a pathologist. I had to give up on my A level as the school where my two youngest children went was constantly closing on Thursdays – my day at the Croydon Tech – for elections and one thing and another.

There's an incident here too that has worried me since that time, and was the main reason that I gave it up again to be truthful: I have a rather inconvenient habit of connecting up the present with the past. I was about to add 'the story of my life' to the end of the last paragraph, then promptly thought of Masha in Chekhov's *Three Sisters*. I'd always wanted to play her while I was still young enough. In those days she was always portrayed as a dreary, sad creature, but I wanted to play her as an amusing girl – witty, funny and attractive. It's probably been done since, but I didn't have the opportunity to do it first (with 'story of my life' wry with a smile). You see, that brings to mind – well, to my mind – Olivier and *Richard III*. The character was always played as an outright villain until Olivier got his hands on him and played him as a humorous man with charisma. This was copied and it became the 'norm'.

To get back to the point, I left my course for a particular reason. There was a young student who made a slightly unpleasant remark to another student. It reminded me of my first husband telling a story of being in a lift at Notting Hill Tube with two or three men who were being rather obstreperous.

Johnny's friend said, 'Look here, you're upsetting my friend' – which I find rather amusing.

Upon which these men turned rather unpleasant – '*Oh,*' one said, 'we're upsetting his friend. – *Are* we upsetting your friend?' It all got rather unpleasant.

And so on until the lift gates opened and Johnny and his friend fled for their lives in opposite directions. We'd always thought this was rather funny.

Out of the blue I said, 'Are you upsetting my friend?' which didn't go down well at all. I tried to explain but wasn't understood. It upset me so much that I never returned.

During my childhood, when you were ill, the fire would be lit in your bedroom, and in the evening various chairs would be brought in and left there so that it could become a sitting room. Your mother and father and sisters would sit with you so that you weren't lonely while you were ill.

There was a funny occasion when I had quinsy – I was sixteen – and the quinsy got rather large so that I couldn't eat at all. I became rather delirious and lost a lot of weight. I can remember hearing my mother and thirteen-year-old Rosebud half laughing outside the bedroom door because in my delirium I was saying, 'Pull my army boots off', but I couldn't speak properly because I had such a swelling on my tonsils which was almost blocking my throat so a rather strange noise came out instead. My father called in a specialist, Mr Mackenzie, who charged about four guineas to come in and lance my abscess, he put a headlight on his forehead like a miner's lamp. He opened his bag and took out a clean scalpel and very gently, with no anaesthetic, he painlessly lanced my abscess – draining a cupful of ghastly 'matter' from it.

My immediate request was for a boiled egg and toast, which I'm very fond of – I still have it for lunch often now.

My poor sister suffered from boils a very short time later, and she had the most awful time. Rosie had a terrible abscess in her left thigh right up in the groin, and her legs became twisted and she couldn't undo them. We didn't have a bedpan, so in order to relieve herself she had to be lifted up on to a pot, which was quite horrid.

We were ill quite a lot, I suppose, probably due to slight malnutrition from war rationing and the fact that there were no fresh fruit imports in those days. Young children didn't know what a banana was! We did occasionally have an orange – if you were under five you were allowed to have one, but Rosebud and I weren't so I suppose we were lacking in vitamin C. You only had the fruit that was in season, although we had our apples; we stored our apples in those days.

When I was sixteen my grandmother died just before my birthday. She was sixty-eight.

It was rather a dreadful shock. She had got cancer of the breast. She didn't go to the doctor but this was because she was a diabetic, and had been since her late thirties. She had treated herself with a diet, not liking the idea of insulin and needles. It was because of her diabetes that Grandma wouldn't have an operation: in those days operations were very dicey for diabetics because the wound could become gangrenous. My grandmother was stoical and resigned to the fact that she was going to die. She even bought a little armchair for my youngest sister's birthday. Lois would have been almost eight, and Grandma said, 'I might as well give it to her now because I shan't be alive for her birthday.' She wasn't.

She took to her bed in the last week or two at home; she was there with my grandfather who was eighty-five and becoming senile, a little childlike. Grandma's sister-in-law Nora happened to pass the house, why I don't know. It wasn't on her usual route to anywhere. As she passed, Aunt Nora heard Grandma screaming. She hurried into the house and found Grandma had broken her leg. Having got out of bed on her right leg to use the commode and her femur had snapped.

The cancer was seated behind a very old scar and one branch had gone to the head of the femur and the other to the right breast. These were secondary tumours, the leg tumour had weakened the leg so much and taken so much strength from it that it had snapped. My grandfather had been trying very clumsily to put her back into bed; it was so painful for her that it made her scream.

Grandma's leg couldn't be mended at all – it was impossible – so she had one of those very uncomfortable rings that go round your hips to hold your body out of the bed and keep the covers off it. My Auntie Marie went to visit her one day and had to sit outside because the doctor was dressing her leg. She heard awful screams and thought, 'That can't be my mother?' Grandma was so brave and stoical.

Fortunately, in a way, because she was a diabetic she fell into a coma and never regained consciousness.

That death affected me a lot because when I went to see

her in the Chapel of Rest, I opened the door, thinking it led into a vestibule, in fact it led straight into the room. And there was my grandmother, facing me.

Because she had been in great pain leading up to her death, all her flesh had fallen away from her face, the mouth was hanging open and the nose had become a very big beak. It was quite a frightening sight.

It was indeed a shock for me, unlike when my grandfather died about three months later from old age, loneliness and disorientation because he'd been taken out of his home – he lived a month with us, then a month with Auntie Marie, then would come back to us. He was staying with us at the end, and he had a slight cold.

I went upstairs to see him one day – 'I'll go and see how Grandfather is,' I said.

I went upstairs, looked at him and he seemed to be asleep, but I sensed he was dead. I went downstairs to my mother and said, 'I think Grandfather's died.'

So she went to see him and he had. Before the funeral he was in his coffin in the drawing room and that was nice; we would say to mother 'may we go and see Grandfather', and we'd all go in and stand round his coffin. We'd stroke his lovely white hair and say, 'Isn't his hair lovely? Look at his lovely skin.' All the blotches had gone. 'Look at his dear little hands,' we'd say, stroking them. There was no fear of death that time because he looked wonderful; and it was a 'good' death, in the sense that he wasn't ill when he died.

That's how we should all die – well. Then we shall all look peaceful and beautiful in our coffins.

Chapter Twelve

Once I'd finished school at seventeen and a half, I decided that, as I wasn't going to university and would have been called up anyway, I'd volunteer for the WRNS. Once you were eighteen your service was chosen for you, so I would have been called up anyway six months later. If you volunteered you could choose which service you went into, if you were called it was their choice. I'd always lived in a port near the sea and loved the water – and I preferred the uniform! It was a nicely shaped jacket, a straight, panelled skirt, a white shirt, black tie, black stockings and a beret – not a forage cap. My complexion wasn't beautiful enough for khaki or Air Force blue. Wrens was the service that most people fancied above the others because of this uniform, and it was also the most senior service.

Although the majority of the American Army was

assembling for the D-Day landings on the Beaches of
Normandy, our Americans stayed on at Wattisham air field
servicing the air-crew and planes that would provide support
for the D-Day landings together with the British and
Canadian forces and the 'Frees'. These consisted of the Free
French, Belgians, Dutch, Danes and Norwegians all eager to
set foot again on their native soil; many of them didn't see
their country again. It is incredible how it was kept secret –
there were posted warnings everywhere during the war years:
'Foolish talk costs lives', 'Walls have ears' and we took notice
of them, nobody passed on what they knew.

How different from today it was; no ferreting out and
making public. I think of us looking at our map, 'England,
the land of the free' we said proudly – oh dear!

The troops of the Empire weren't conscripted, those countries declared war a day or so after our government did and
they had their own governments.

So, having defended my country from those who would
decry our old empire, I would return to my small life.

Having received my papers from the WRNS upon my
enlistment and a travel warrant to take me to Scotland for
basic training, I thought it would be a good idea to visit the
last young man I'd been friendly with, Terry Hurst, in
Bridgnorth in Shropshire where he was stationed with the
RAF.

I dropped in for a day to see him, spending the night
on my own at a boarding house, and then continued on to
HMS *Spartiate* at Balloch – a training camp on the shores of
Loch Lomond, which sounds incredibly romantic, but wasn't.

On the train journey I wrote a letter to Mother telling her

about the red earth of Somerset as I hadn't much else to write about. I'd only left home two days before. Rosebud must have told me about Mother's reaction to it and other letters following from Balloch.

The three weeks' basic training was physically one of the hardest work experiences. I had always remembered it as *six* weeks – it certainly felt like it – until I found my old WRNS Certificate of Service the other day. If you had volunteered and you didn't like it, you could leave – you could get out after basic training. But I had too much pride to go home with my tail between my legs, so I stuck it out. Particularly as I would have been called up six months later and would have to endure it all over again as soon as I was eighteen.

We did dreadful route marches along the south shores of Loch Lomond, but even they weren't as bad as getting up at five o'clock in the morning for kitchen duty – scrubbing floors or scouring pans and doing all the filthy, physical work which I'd never really done before. I'd washed up, laid fires and made beds, but I hadn't got down on my hands and knees scrubbing. Ever since then I've had no desire to return to the 'Bonnie Banks of Loch Lomond'! It would bring back unpleasant memories.

After the basic training I was sent to HMS *Pembroke* a land-base at Chatham, Kent. I hoped I might train to be an aircraft mechanic – I wasn't very mechanical so it was probably just as well I was trained as a cinema operator to show films on both 16mm and 35mm projectors.

I did have a horrible experience when I had to show the newsreel films that came out of Belsen after the war; it was extremely shocking for a girl of eighteen. They were the very first that had come out of Belsen, and suddenly there I was showing them – as I was the only projectionist at Argentinny I had to show those films. We were a very innocent generation in a way, so it was unbelievable to us that anybody could behave in that way. I can still see those figures, wandering aimlessly, almost sideways, like skeletons in those striped pyjamas. The heaps of bodies and the thinness of them was so absolutely shocking.

One evening during my two-week training period I went out with a group of four Wrens in Rochester, where we lived in our 'Wrennery'. We decided we wanted to go for a drink but we were all young – seventeen or eighteen – and not long out of school. I looked a lot older, as I wore Max Factor Pan-Cake to cover my complexion.

At that time one didn't go into pubs without a man as an escort, so there we were, this group of young girls walking around the town looking for a suitable pub or hotel, but each time we passed one we dare not go in. It became quite ridiculous, and eventually we decided that we must all summon up the courage to enter the next one. We stopped outside a hotel with a revolving door, whereupon one of us Paddy Gawk-Rogers, very purposefully marched in – but we didn't. She swung through the revolving door and with barely a pause came straight out the other side.

We fell about laughing, and I laughed so much that I wet my navy-blue standard-issue drawers, so we all had to go back to the Wrennery!

On 13 October 1944 I was posted up to Scotland again, this time to HMS *Armadillo* in Ardentinny – a combined army and naval base – known as 'combined ops' – on the shore of another loch, Loch Long. I was the only cinema operator and my job was to show 16mm newsreels and training films on how to use the landing craft and tanks that had been used for the D-Day landings, and how to survive wherever you landed. Jimmy Hanley, who was to become a big English filmstar, appeared in some of them.

Not long after I arrived at the base, I went to a Halloween party in the village of Blairmore, just down the lock-side where I learned to dance Scottish reels and ducked for apples. I met a group of young boys and girls from Glasgow and I used to go out with them sometimes on my leaves there. I became friendly with them and spent weekends staying at one of their homes in Glasgow and going out with that dear boy, I was very grateful to him for drawing me into their circle and being so kind to me. They were all very friendly and made me part of them, I hadn't yet formed a particular friendship in those early months at Ardentinny.

I wrote to Mother on the train to Glasgow saying how beautiful the countryside was, how red the earth was. Then I heard that Mother had exclaimed 'Oh, another of June's descriptive letters!' and that stopped me writing many more. I still thought of her and her passion for hats. I found a small one in apple green in Glasgow on one of my weekend leaves, that I bought her for her birthday in March, green being her favourite colour. Several years later I got up early to be at the head of the queue to capture a dark emerald coloured fur-felt hat that I'd seen in the window of a store in Bath, marked down to 50p. I really cared about Mother even though I was loved by her the least. She had a rapport with Rosebud and was always happy being with her. Whilst staying with me for her last Christmas when Rosebud and I were living in flats opposite each other in South Croydon, 'Mother,' I said, 'why don't you go and see Rosie, you get on better with her.' She didn't deny it but in a surprised but completely accepting way said, 'You're not jealous, are you?'

'No, because it's true.'

There's a lump in my throat as I write this now, but it didn't affect me then. I was being matter-of-fact about what was obvious.

Most of the Wrens worked in teams, but Babs and I worked alone. She was the gardener on the base, where she grew vegetables for the kitchen. She had a little stone hut with a couple of benches and a stove. Babs and I became great friends; again, she was familiar to me with her straight dark-brown hair, brown eyes and rosy cheeks.

A group of us would often go for walks; we'd put ten shillings in the kitty and climb the mountain behind Ardentinny, passing the wishing well and on down to Loch Eck, where we ate boiled eggs, toast and cake, and finished off drinking whisky and chasers at the bar until the kitty ran dry. We were singing merrily as we walked all the way back again, fortunately the way back was all down hill. Ten bob went a long way in those days.

I'd made friends with Gertrude Logan, like me she was the only one in her category. She was the gardener and I had been on the walk to Loch Eck with some of the girls from my hut whom I liked and got on well with but they worked together in their jobs, so I only saw them off-duty. One of them went on leave to get married to her sailor fiancé. I can see her sitting in her top bunk crying because she was missing him, we tried to comfort her but didn't succeed, 'You don't know what it's like!' she wept. We didn't, we were virginal.

Then there was Bunny, constantly sitting up in her lower bunk next to mine, bumping her head on the top exclaiming, 'Sod it!' This was a very rude swear for us but said in her cultivated accent, sounded very funny. In that accent it didn't sound crude. The top bunks were the coveted ones open to the air but you had to wait to be elevated as there was a queue for them according to the length of your stay. One queued for everything in those days, queuing became a national characteristic.

I had a week's leave at Christmas and went home. Two years before Raoul had sent me that Christmas card, this year again there was nothing from him. I was still hoping. Mother was rather sad as she missed her mother whom she used to visit every day. Rosebud and Lois were both at school but still sang with Mother in the evenings, sometimes played the piano themselves. They brought their friends home and Johnny Cameron and Bernard would usually visit at weekends, so the house still had life.

Rosebud had two good friends: Pat Hamblin had moved into Number 33 after we moved out and became a constant visitor. Her mother had run off with the married Austrian baker at the top of the road – he sold unusual cakes like Apple Strudel. So, Pat being motherless, became like a daughter to Mother and a sister to Rosebud, so much so that three years later Pat, who was training to be a nurse, was asleep on the sofa in our house one night and woke to see

Rosebud standing in front of the sideboard on the other side of the room. Rosebud faded from her view from the top and bottom of her body leaving her stomach till last and then Rosebud disappeared, she was on the train from London nursing a very painful stomach ache and longing to be home.

Eileen, her school friend, played duets with her. They met again about ten years or more ago when Eileen moved close to Croydon and they picked up their friendship from where they had left off.

We had a merry Christmas at home and I went back on that long journey to Scotland which had taken up two days of my week. On that overcrowded dim and eerily-lit night train back to Glasgow I was sitting on the floor in the corridor amongst a row of servicemen. I woke up with my head on the shoulder of a soldier who paid me a compliment, 'You've got lovely knees'!

It must have been cold that winter in Ardentinny but I remember only the sunny days and my 18th birthday in February. I celebrated that in the hut with the others. It would have been too cold for us to climb to the inn on Loch Eck.

I would often see Lieutenant Patrick Sullivan Tailyour whom I'd met at a dance in Dunoon, our nearest town reached by bus. He was Irish, a submariner and a rather vigorous dancer. I remember him throwing me around the dancefloor with us both singing:

You've got to accentuate the positive,
Eliminate the negative,
Latch on to the affirmative,
Don't mess with Mr Inbetween.

His submarine would tie up at Ardentinny and I'd go aboard to drink pink gin in the officers' mess – two small benches either side of a narrow table – and once he let me survey the view from the periscope. He had a sensitive side, he wrote poetry and wrote me several poems. I wish I hadn't lost them, I can't even remember their sentiment, expressing love I think. They were well-written I remember that.

Patrick was posted away, probably to the waters surrounding Japan.

The end of the European war was to come, on 8 May 1945. This bought with it enormous happiness. The lights of the streets and houses came on again – we were no longer a dark fortress of a country.

VE day was celebrated. I couldn't get leave to go to London but we had fireworks, food and parties on the landing craft that were attached to the base. After that joy I was to be brought down to earth. I was the only one who could show the news reels. They were full of the liberation by our Army camps in Germany – Belsen and Buchenwald.

While at HMS *Armadillo* Ardentinny, and two years after my first quinsy, another appeared in the same place. I was taken to the sickbay, but after a day they decided that they hadn't the facilities to deal with it, so I had to be transferred to the Royal Naval Hospital at Newton Mearns, a suburb of Glasgow. I was taken first by launch across Loch Long to Greenock, and then by ambulance for the rest of the journey. The ambulance journey was a wretched experience. I was thrown about, bumping over cobbles, pot-holes and tramlines so violently that it caused a non-surgical quinsy removal – it burst en route!

The quinsy promptly re-appeared and again this one burst of its own accord. The young doctor at the naval hospital got a pair of tongs and tried to nip it to burst it, which was excruciatingly painful. After that it was decided that my tonsils must be removed, this was done in a terribly bad way – they were guillotined, which left great holes in the back of my throat. I went into the operating theatre, having had what seemed like twenty injections in my tonsils, sitting with a rubber apron on and was talking to the surgeon the whole time he was removing them.

Although I hadn't heard from Raoul for three years, I was still waiting for him. Rosemary vaguely remembers him coming to the house once when I wasn't there. There must have been a letter asking me to see him in London. I must have arranged it, taken an overnight train, been met at Euston. 'Surely not, I was always there' I said and then I wondered if he'd appeared when I was in the WRNS but most of what happened on that weekend is a blank. I know I took leave to go to London, the days are a blank.

I remember only three restaurants, three tables and a bedroom. It is as if the tables are isolated from each other and not connected to their surroundings at all – no leaving, no journeying, no arriving, no being met at a station, no arriving at a restaurant, just three meals, one after the other.

The first table was in Genarro's near Piccadilly Circus. I remember going down the stairs and sitting at a table with this stranger who seemed to know the reason for my three years of silence from Raoul. Her attitude towards me was so odd, matter-of-fact impersonal, as if I were a casual acquaintance to whom she was relating her life story – to this dummy – I must have seemed like one as I sat looking, listening to her as she talked on and on about herself and how she had escaped from Jersey when the Germans occupied the Channel Islands.

I remember the facts but not the words, except for a solitary sentence: 'I went to church and prayed to God. I promised him that if he brought Raoul safely back to me I would give £10 to the poor box, and I did.' I was so shocked, But you can't bribe God, I thought. I said nothing.

I knew I was in Pattisserie Valerie. It seems I was sitting by the window at a table with a plate of cream cakes on it. I suppose I remember because cream cakes were impossible to get just after the war. I don't know who was there with me.

It was evening, I was sitting in a small, ordinary restaurant. Each of the restaurants was near Piccadilly Circus, where I'd first been with Raoul on that day he took me to Tolworth to stay with his mother and sister. Raoul was on my left, Rosa on my right and opposite me Raoul's friend Jean Palissau. He had been invited to lighten the tension between the other three, to take my mind off what was happening. He was a handsome young Frenchman and a Lieutenant in the British Army. I knew somehow that Raoul was a captain. I must have seen the three pips on his epaulettes. I remember what we ate because Raoul asked me if I liked it. This is the only time I remember seeing his face.

'Yes,' I said.

'It was horse,' he informed me.

'Oh, was it?'

I had no reaction to this. I was utterly numb.

And that's all of that scrap of conversation that has stayed with me. It is the one memory I have of Raoul during the whole day. If I hadn't remembered that, I wouldn't be able to tell you that he was there at all.

Finally, the bedroom belonged to Jean Palissau. It was his room in a renting house in King's Cross and I suppose I was expected to stay there alone. He pulled the bed down from what looked like a cupboard – upright and pinned to the wall. But Jean stayed with me, and then I was in bed with him and we were both naked – I with my head on his left shoulder, and he with his arms around me. He told me that his name was very common in France, like John Smith, he said. If it had been Lebrun he would have been John Brown, like my brother John Peter. Rosa Roche was a pretty name; I'd have liked a name like that. I asked my mother once why she called me June. I've never liked it. 'It was a popular name at the time.' Junes should be fair-haired with blue eyes.

'You won't tell Raoul will you?'

'Of course not!'

There was nothing to tell, and I wasn't to see Raoul again.

We were all invited to Raoul and Rosa's wedding, but nobody went. I think it would have been expensive for my parents to travel and stay in London. I certainly didn't want to go.

I wonder if, when I reached Glasgow on the Sunday after that disastrous weekend, I took the train to Gourock, and then the ferry across the loch to Dunoon or Blairmore or whether I got off at Greenock where our old herring drifter would be waiting and got in the hold smelling of fish. It would have been a fitting end.

'I haven't said thanks for that lovely weekend, those two days of heaven you helped me to spend!' The thought has sent me into a fit of laughter, and I've always said that when you can laugh at something that once upset you, you're over it, you're cured – and about time too, you might say!

I went to Greenock on that old herring drifter and then took the train to Glasgow to stay with Bill Walker's aunt for my leave on the weekend of Raoul's wedding. That night of the wedding I went to bed, fell asleep and woke up the next morning and it was as if it had never been. I took up my life again as before and went back in Ardentinny. One day I was walking past the tennis court and noticed a handsome young officer in his tennis whites playing rather well. We were together until we were both posted elsewhere in August 1945.

The captain of the base had taken to visiting the garden and having chats with Babs. One time, she had invited her young man, Colin and me for cocoa on our morning break. We were all huddled in this tiny hut drinking cocoa smoking, laughing and joking when suddenly the captain appeared at the doorway. We were all stunned, jumped to our feet and saluted. We weren't doing anything wrong but the captain had picked a rather unfortunate moment to call in for a chat, and it was somewhat embarrassing for Babs!

Colin was an only child. We went to stay with his parents, Tilly and Reg – it was a significant action then, 'meeting the parents'. We were to stay at their home in Frizinghall, a suburb of Bradford (pronounced 'Bratford' by those in the know). They were indeed an odd couple, not well matched I would say, but seemingly peaceful and content. Tilly spoke in a high voice and laughed accordingly. She loved listening to classical music, although nobody played any instruments, just the gramophone, a record player to those of today – or should it be a CD player? Colin and Tilly would listen to it together. Tilly was also a rather good tennis player, as was Colin, and they played tennis together. I accepted this with equanimity, as was my wont.

Tilly slept in a double bed placed diagonally across the bedroom, quite unusual at the time. This was given over to me during my stay, which must have been a week's leave that Colin and I managed to take together. She cooked on a gas-ring placed in the hearth – a strange quirk in what I suppose was a dining room-cum-sitting room-cum-kitchen for all I know. I remember sitting in an armchair close to the gas-ring while Tilly and Colin sat on the sofa, all of us listening to some piece of classical music, possibly orchestral. When I cast my memory back, Reggie seems to be missing from that scene.

Reggie was a journalist with the *Yorkshire Post* who also compiled crossword puzzles. He was the gentle sort of Yorkshireman who looked like J. B. Priestley (whose play *Time and the Conways* is a favourite of mine, with its wonderfully satisfying part of Kay Conway which I played in my days at Colchester rep). My memories of Reg are of meeting him on the landing, when he held me tightly in his arms and exclaimed, 'Flaming June!' I hasten to add that this was spoken as a compliment, not a slur upon my character. The other one is of an old-fashioned, comfortable, brown and smoky pub where Reg, with his good-humoured face, sat smoking his pipe with Colin and me, with no sign of Tilly.

Reg and Colin shared a twin-bedded room across the landing from Tilly, who slept in her double bed in all her singleness.

To use a delicate phrase, we had become lovers. One's attitude to life changes after that, so it is a move that should be taken with caution but seldom is.

Upon our return to Ardentinny we had no opportunity for further love-making until Colin and his friend were posted to Troon on the west coast of Scotland, leaving Babs and I forlorn. I wrote to Colin every day but learning a lesson from Mother I left out descriptions of the country-side, which I might add was very beautiful. Suffolk isn't flat like Essex, not if you've had cycling experience around it, but its hills cannot compare to the Scottish lowlands. I got a weekend pass and went to visit Colin in Troon, staying as his wife in some small hotel; that was quite a common occurrence during the war as you might not see the other person again for some time, there was no certainty of that during the war. Attitudes were turned around and changed thereafter. Most of my friends at home only experienced the delights of marriage on their wedding day, their true first night. In fact very different from now when marriage is becoming out of fashion. To return to Troon, I had begun to notice that Colin's favourite habit was 'the pub', he was at home there. He had got used to it with his father Reggie's pipe, his cigarettes, their pints and conversation. Reg didn't seem very interested in classical music nor playing tennis but he was a bit stout so, maybe, in his slender youth he had met Tilly at the tennis club.

I have to make myself eat nowadays but then I wanted lunch not a sweet sherry or gin and orange standing at the bar, that wouldn't have augured well for our marriage, not with Father in mind. Colin, however, never got obviously inebriated and apart from that I enjoyed being with him, he was never bad tempered or argumentative and was interesting to talk to and listen to. He was a teacher in Suffolk. I found this out from Reggie once while on tour with Johnny, my first husband, when he was in the all-male cast of *Seagulls Over Sorrento*. I visited Reggie in Bradford, living with a younger woman, a distant cousin, Tilly having died, her bedroom stacked with newspaper. Colin didn't approve of his father's liaison.

I continued to write my interminable love letter when I was back from Troon in early August after Colin was posted again, and I was posted to Somerset.

A group of us would go out riding – for me who had never sat on a horse, this meant that I was assisted into the saddle, given the reins, had my feet inserted into the stirrups and sent off from the stables to the old Roman road that ran through the fields and was covered with grass. Blackie, my small horse, knew he was in control and would lag behind the rest while I bumped away on his back until they were out of sight, then he'd stop and refuse to move. I'd dismount, tie him up and lie down on the bank until the others returned.

One time, Blackie, who went willingly back to the stables, was behaving himself and I found the rhythm of the trot.

Glen, a Canadian pilot, taught me to ride Western style, reins in left hand, right hand ready to shoot, throw a lasso or clutch on to the saddle!

'Look, look,' I shouted in excitement, 'I've found the rhythm of the trot!' Glen helped Blackie into what seemed to me to be a gallop; it was probably a canter. I think Blackie enjoyed himself, I didn't, I lost my hair ribbon. I was too busy holding on to the saddle to be able to save it from being blown off my head. We didn't bother with hard hats. I wore a pair of fawn breeches that I'd bought for my 'Dig For Victory' Saturdays, hoeing fields of sugar beet in Suffolk when I was sixteen, a blue Harris Tweed jacket from a suit I owned, long fawn socks and brown suede flat shoes. I'd bought the breeches from Millets, which was managed by Pat Hamblin's father. You have to dress the part! Glen told me he was half Red Indian half Canadian. That was the term he used and he seemed proud of that blood in his veins. They were halcyon days in those peaceful fields in Somerset.

It wasn't long after that I auditioned for one of the leading parts in a WRNS production, a play called *Call It a Day* – and there have been times when I've thought maybe I should have done!

We toured various southern commands, bolstering morale. I played the elder sister Cath Hilton, a young girl who was madly in love with a married artist. Olivia de Havilland had played her in the film in the Thirties. I believe the play was a romantic comedy but I took the whole thing very seriously. I too was a young girl, and I knew what it was like to be in love! To my horror the audience of sailors used to fall about laughing, and I just couldn't understand why.

My character, in particular, used to get a lot of laughs, and I'd come off stage very upset, complaining, 'They're so insensitive!' Unwittingly, I had played the part the right way – I was far too serious to 'play it for laughs'. But that's why it worked: it came from truth, and I was to understand more of that later on in my theatre training.

Call It a Day had made me think I might like to act. It was lovely to get approval, applause, and it was a nice life; on tour we would stay at different Wrenneries and visit the officers' mess to have drinks after the performances.

I loved being in the Wrens; I had an interesting time. I was fortunate that I was never in any danger of enemy action, but the European war was over before I left the Wrens – the lights had gone up on London. I arrived at HMS *Heron*, the naval airbase at Yeovilton in Somerset, a few days before the atom bombs were dropped on Japan. Colin rang me that night.

I hitchhiked from Yeovilton to London on VJ Day. Strangely, I can't recall if I was with a group, but I know I stayed at the Services Club that night. I went to the Mall, which of course was crowded. Everyone was cheering, laughing, dancing. At one point I was with a group of French soldiers; one moment I was wearing one of their navy berets with the red pompom, the next, my own. I can't describe the incredible rapture we all felt. We had been at war for six years, all through my teens. Suddenly the war was over. The Japanese had surrendered, which no one had ever expected they would, not, of course, the Japanese who would commit hara-kiri rather than face capture.

American, British and German scientists had collaborated to perfect the atom bomb. The atom had been split, that unimaginable action that defied nature and released a devastating power. 'The atom is the smallest indivisible particle' – or so we had learnt at school. No one knew what the horrifying effects of that action would be. Emperor Hirohito had said that if one foreign foot was set upon the Japanese mainland, every prisoner of war would be killed. Two bombs were dropped instead – one on Hiroshima, one over Nagasaki.

Siegfried Sassoon's wonderful poem, 'Everyone Sang', written at the end of the Great War, described the nation's joy as a spontaneous outburst of singing. This is exactly how we felt.

The Wrennery I was living in now was called Rosebank, a beautiful old brick house in the idyllic village of Queen Camel a few miles from the naval base where we worked. We slept in shared rooms of four and I was with three others. I was very happy there for the year to come. As VJ Day had happened ten days after I arrived, the following eleven months before I was de-mobbed were peaceful. I showed films for entertainment at night as well as for training.

The night I arrived, the others in my room took me through our side gate across the lane which led up to the church, and in through the side door of the pub opposite. We drank the local apple cider known as 'rough cider' or 'scrumpy'. I thought that it would be almost non-alcoholic, but suddenly I was on my own, wandering through fields on a warm August night. I never found those fields, nor drank scrumpy, again.

There was a free and easy air about the base on my first working day. Arriving at the cinema box, I was greeted by three other Wrens.

'What's your name?' one of them asked me.

'I'm June.'

'Oh no, you can't be.' They were laughing.

I looked bemused.

She continued, 'Because I'm Jean and she's Joan and I'm Jane.'

We didn't become bosom pals, although Jean was a very pleasant Scottish girl who was the senior Wren. Joan was a pretty blonde northerner who was engaged to be married and longed for her wedding day because then she would be able to wear black stockings with a red suit – something that would look 'tarty' on a single girl. She thought Jane was very forthright and practical, and was worried about marrying her fiancé, a South African, and living in Johannesburg, as she would have to employ servants. She'd rather do her own housework, she said to me.

I got on with them very well, there was never a moment of dissension. We chatted, made toast in front of a small electric fire, smoked our cigarettes in the office beside the projection box where the film was stored, and never considered it posed much of a fire risk. Our duties at the base entailed showing major entertainment films at night to entertain the ratings, on 35mm projectors with carbons – you had to be constantly watching them, changing them and readjusting them.

We checked the films during the day. Each reel showing twenty minutes of film was placed on a spool, one end of the reel was threaded through an empty spool and the film rewound while running our finger along the edge of the film, as we would have to check for broken sprockets. These were cut out and the clean edges glued together. If these were missed and the film oiled inside the projector, it could cause a very dangerous fire. My uncle – Father's half-brother, Leonard – was killed in just such a fire before I was born. He was an early cinema operator in the 1920s.

It's odd to think I can actually work on both sides of the camera now – I haven't shown a film for years, though. I did learn a lesson about electricity at the time. I was making some toast on a metal fork in front of this old-fashioned fire, which was heated by a long coiled wire like a spring, wound lengthwise along grooves in the fireproof back. A bit of the wire dropped from its groove and I tried to put it back with my toasting fork. I was very surprised when the wire went black and fell in little pieces on the shelf. I learnt that you shouldn't touch a live wire with a metal object, thanks Mother!

I've never trusted electricity. I was still learning by experience.

Once I was passing the time of day with Olive, my friend from across the road in Folkestone when I lived there years later, and coming back into the house I discovered that my spin dryer had been on so long that it was sending out smoke signals. I put two pairs of wellington boots on – one pair on my hands and the other on my feet – before daring to switch the spin dryer off.

My second husband, Bob, once asked me if I knew how to treat a person for electric shock.

'Yes, why?' I asked him.

'I'm just going to lower the mains supply down a foot or so.'

'You'll be burnt to a crisp before I get my wellies on!' I said.

He survived and completed the job of making his fusebox cupboard.

Bob was known as 'Bobby Beading' at one time, christened thus by one of my eldest daughter Louise's friends, Carl. Bob covered any ill-fitting joins in his many DIY projects with a wooden strip known as beading. I could extend this book hugely by adding several chapters on his conversions: for example, he once changed a simple bathroom cupboard beside the basin into a chute for soiled clothing – to be slung in, landing in a dirty-clothes basket in the utility room below, beside the washing machine. Actually, that was one of his better ideas.

Back in the cinema box, Jean, Joan, Jane and I all longed for red. I wanted red shoes, and I got them in Yeovil; unfortunately they were Brevitts in a dark red leather, and I wanted a pair of vermilion ones by Joyce, as they were a nicer shape. There were very few to be had, and as soon as it was on the grapevine that a consign had arrived at the shoe shop a queue formed. I was not at the head of it that time.

The WRNS did not provide their personnel with naval-issue bras, pants, stockings or nightwear, but issued us with clothing 'chits' instead. The chits were accepted in the shops in lieu of clothing coupons, with different values for different items. We always applied for pyjama chits, as they garnered you the highest number of coupons, eight. Armed with these, we bought civilian clothing: dresses, shoes, skirts. The naval clothing store never seemed to question why our pyjamas wore out so fast.

I stayed at Yeovilton until the following autumn and enjoyed my time there. Amongst the group of pilots that I showed my 16mm training films to was an American, Joseph Cowling, known as 'Smoky' – an allusion to the cowling on a chimney. I fell in love again.

He'd been one of the Eagle Squadron, those flyers who'd left America to fight against Germany by joining the RAF before America entered the war and who were stationed at Martlesham for a time. (It was at Martlesham that I saw the bomb fall from the bay of a German fighter bomber when I was fourteen.) He was easy to love. He took me out to dinner at 'The Mermaid Hotel' in Yeovil, where the price ceiling for dinner was five shillings (twenty-five pence), as it was at every hotel or restaurant at the time. I found out later that he was married. I used to visit the intelligence officer to have a cocoa with him. Talking of Smoky, he said, 'You know he's married?'

'He's not!' Instant denial.

'Oh yes, I met him in London last weekend going into a restaurant. She's fair-haired, small, lovely. She's Swedish.'

Smoky was being posted away soon so I said nothing just went and stood outside the air station and waved my group off. They were probably laughing at me as they vanished into the distance. I had known them all, as I had showed them the training film of how to land on an aircraft carrier – a hazardous undertaking. Some were killed attempting it in a rough sea. That's how I'd met 'Smoky Joe'.

I had a very lovely friend, Verity Waterlow, who was a photographer. We hitched to Downside Abbey, where the swans came out to ring the bell for their meal. I think one of the young ratings with us was quite keen on me – I had dinner with him not long ago near Berkeley Square at the Royal Naval Club; he had become a clerk of the court at Marylebone.

I had a room close to another lovely girl called Betty. She was the daughter of an Earl. She was talking to me one day about her social difficulties – she had to refuse anyone's advances. 'It's alright for you, you see, you can go out with anybody – I can't.' She asked me if I would introduce her from then on as the Lady Elizabeth. So, at the next party, I did just that. Smoky Joe said, 'You're a snob.' I explained that that was how she had asked me to present her, I think he understood, I did.

I knew several young officers, and there was one in particular, who was an Irishman, Stephen John Horgan. I met him coming from the cinema box, he was on his motorbike. He'd sing me Irish songs and he was very bright and sweet, and rode around on his motorbike all the time. Occasionally, when I was up top in my projection box, I'd lean out of the window and wave to Stephen John Horgan as he sped past. It wasn't long before I was up on 'captain's defaulters' with 'off-caps' – off came your Wren cap and in you went to see the captain. I had been accused of waving at passers-by from my projection box. I think I had the courage to say that we only waved at people we knew but we were reprimanded anyway – as though we were leaning out waving to strangers, like prostitutes on the Amsterdam canals!

A friend I was to make while at the Young Vic Company – he played Theseus to my Hippolyta and we used to vie with each other with our voices – told me once that while he was with a Scots Company at the end of the war some of his group went into Belsen. They were so appalled by what they saw that they took their rifles and clubbed some German guards to death. Butch, who is probably in his nineties now and still worked in the theatre the last time I heard, always appeared to be so untouched by what he had gone through during the war, despite having seen so much.

I did have a friend who'd been in the merchant navy, a young boy, no older than myself, about seventeen or so, who was the only one I knew who was affected by it – he ended up in a psychiatric hospital. He'd been shipwrecked and rescued three times while people drowned in the water around him in the Atlantic ocean. If you think about a boy of seventeen going to sea and being torpedoed, then rescued, and then going off on another ship and it happening again, and again – it was no wonder he suffered afterwards.

The men who went through these experiences didn't talk about them. I knew an Air Force officer who'd been shot down and had the most dreadful limp – his leg went down and then out, so he was visibly very awkward. But the point was that you ignored this completely, and as a young girl of seventeen I would wait for him to come and open the car door and let me out and then shut it after me. Then I'd let him open the door into the restaurant or pub, or wherever we were going, because I wouldn't offend him by treating him as if he were, well, what was the title of that play I was in

at the Royal Court? – 'just a little bit less than normal'. Karl
Johnson played my crippled son.

'I'm a cripple', he complained.

'You're not a cripple, son!'

'What am I then?'

'You're . . . just a little bit less than normal.'

Chapter Thirteen

I was demobbed on 1 July 1946 and left the WRNS, returning to Ipswich on 28 July. The first week I felt incredibly tired, lying on the sofa most of the day, hardly able to move. I decided to go to an osteopath for treatment to see if he could get my energy back for me. Mr Pearce lived not far away, on Cauldwell Hall Road. I often wondered if he had been fully trained and whether he had studied at the School of Osteopathy, where I had wanted to train, but I do know that he gave me the best treatment I have ever had.

I left his practice with a light heart and a spring in my step; ready to look for work of some description – I had no idea what.

Roma was living back in Ilford and Eva was with the American forces in Germany, but I still had two of my friends – Peggy was working in the laboratory at Fison's and

Pauline was a secretary in some office or other. Neither of them had been called up. I didn't question it then, but it puzzles me now. Bill, Pauline's beau, was in the RAF, where he was to stay until retiring in his forties, having been given a permanent commission. He had wanted to become a pilot but he was too good at maths, so he was sent to be trained as a navigator.

It was good to be with the family again and enjoy my time while I looked for work. I loved being able to go to the sea again, walk on the pebbles, swim in the sea. The waves were often strong on the east coast and it was invigorating to swim against them. Fit again from Mr Pearce's ministrations, I was happy to be with all the family as we joined together for expeditions to Felixstowe or the countryside. Off we'd go, three cars in a line, on our way to the rendezvous. Invariably only two would arrive and one would vanish. The Browns' car never got lost but I expect Father was heading the queue.

'Where the hell are they? I'll go and find them, Harry. You stay here, in case they turn up,' Uncle would pacify Father. It was always John or Colin who was driving the missing last car. I expect passengers were mixed up, a Brown in a Templey vehicle and vice versa.

Usually it turned out that the lost sheep had taken a different route – maybe the country way, known as 'the pretty way' by Mother – strictly against instructions. The rest of the mixed-up collection would react according to their temperament – a tutting here and a tapping of a foot there, one gazing at the sea, one smoking a cigarette – that would be me.

Once we were all assembled, not necessarily in an entirely happy frame of mind, we'd unpack the various picnics and towels, swimming costumes and blankets, and troop down to the beach.

On the first of these outings, we made our way down the beach and the cloth was already spread and the biscuit tins containing food unpacked, but then I said, looking around, 'Oh, we can't stay here, it's far too crowded!' So tins up, cloths and blankets lifted, we traipsed back to our cars parked by the prom – no yellow lines or directions to a car park in those days – and off we drove to the next beach up the coast.

After following the same procedure two or three times, we finally arrived at a lovely deserted beach and were greeted with a big sign: 'DANGER! MINES!' Disheartened, we stood. Suddenly, a man strode by with his towel over his shoulder and, seeing us there, remarked cheerfully, 'I don't take any notice of that, I swim here every day.'

We followed our leader on to the beach, all of us disappearing straight into the sea to swim and frolic, leaving Mother with the unpacked picnic and piles of outer clothing as usual. As she sat she was idly running her hands through the sand, sifting it through her fingers when she suddenly uncovered a round tin thing – she didn't say a word, she quietly got up, gathered our clothes and belongings together and moved further up the beach away from it. After our swim we ran up the beach to Mother and got dried and dressed ourselves. Only when we finally left the beach did she say 'I discovered a mine!' We hadn't noticed she'd moved!

Another time the motley crew was picnicking in a field.

The cloth was down, with the various shapes of biscuit tin on it, cups at the ready, as Uncle Billy attempted to light the Primus stove, Colin assisting, in order to boil the kettle. It would not light. Uncle was getting into a bit of a strop when a family appeared, out for a walk in the country, and stopped at our cloth. We were having our picnic across the footpath! Up we got and removed it, but for some unknown reason put it straight back down again in the same place. I don't think we could have been concentrating; perhaps we were distracted by Uncle's lack of success with his Primus stove. I don't think we ever got that tea.

These jaunts were never the jolliest, but they afforded us great amusement in times to come. 'Do you remember when Mother . . .?' and 'What about that footpath?' and 'Uncle Billy and his Primus stove!' Shrieks of laughter!

Activities with my friends were less troubled. Pauline, Peggy and I were all fancy-free – Bill was away in the RAF, Colin was in the Far East and Peggy had no boyfriend in particular, so we wasted no time commiserating over our woes – we didn't have any. Mother said to me two or three years later, 'I liked you better before you went to that Old Vic School – you were a plump, jolly girl!' I wasn't fat just nicely covered. I wish I were now.

Pauline and I would go dancing or to the pictures, or just sit in her house talking to Mrs Russell, eating her special ginger cake known as parkin – a Yorkshire recipe. She and her husband Reggie Russell had Yorkshire roots and were very proud of them and kept up with this tradition of parkin – not 'ginger cake'! They were a traditional family – the girls refused to get up on Christmas Day until their mother played and sang 'Christians Awake, Salute the Happy Morn'. For me, after Micie was gone, there was a great deal of kindness in them, and I will always remember them with gratitude for gathering me into their family; Pam taking me out with Pauline. They're all gone now.

I saw Peggy most frequently, because Bill, a colleague in her lab, had a friend who owned a boat that we could borrow – an old 32-footer with brown sails. Although they were brown they were known as red I think. We used to sail at the weekends at Pin Mill, on the south shore of the River Orwell, downriver from Ipswich. I wasn't allowed to steer with the wooden tiller aft, because on my first attempt Bill and Peggy had to fend the boat off a buoy which I was steering straight towards! I was relegated to pulling on the ropes and ducking every time the boom swung round, plus making tea and frying sausages in the galley.

They were lovely days. One night after our sail, Bill and I were on the boat alone. We'd had our supper of bread and fried sausages in the galley while we were at anchor, then Bill rowed us to the shore. The water was fluorescent – I've never seen it before or since, but the light flew from the blades of the oars as they dipped in and out. Bill and I were never more than friends but it was still a romantic moment.

I revisited Pin Mill not long ago, after attending a tree-planting ceremony at the new site of the High School with my sisters Rosemary and Lois, and Mary Cadman, where Eva planted a sweet chestnut tree in memory of her family, the Nussbaums, which translates as nut trees. Pin Mill was unchanged – the Butt and Oyster Inn still stands at the water's edge. We sat there, watching the boats on the river and the dinghies pull up on 'the hard' before our return journey to London.

To complete my return to health, either wittingly or not, Father decided to hire a car and driver to take the family to Cornwall to stay for a fortnight – twice as long as our usual holidays, and different scenery. Father was earning quite well, still at the yeast factory, British Fermentation Products Ltd, and there was talk of him being sent to Singapore to expand the business, and taking us with him. That was an exciting prospect.

Off we went in our comfortable car, with a better driver than Father at the wheel. We stopped for lunch at a waterside hotel to give the driver a break, as well as us all having a meal on the long journey from Ipswich to Penzance. There were no motorways to shorten the time – it took hours. I tasted real spaghetti Napolitana for the first course, not the tinned variety – that was all we were used to. It was absolutely delicious – the taste of the sauce was better than I'd ever known. It must have been – otherwise, why would I remember it so vividly?

At the hotel in Penzance were two friends from London, also holidaying – Aumi Shapiro was a former actor who'd just been demobbed from the army, and Jack Zussman from the navy. He was about to go to St Edmund's College to read mathematics at Cambridge.

Rosebud and I went out with them quite a lot, which was more interesting for us at the ages of sixteen and nineteen than being with our parents and ten-year-old Lois, or 'Lolo'. We all had nicknames – I was Juniper, Junipegs or Juno;

Rosemary had been Rosebud, Buddy or Bud. Buddy was hastily discarded when the Americans arrived in Suffolk and we found that 'buddy' was their equivalent term for 'mate'. Father, Henry, was always Harry, and his name for my mother was not Louie, as was usual, but he pronounced it Loy. Thinking about it, I imagine it was Loie.

Rosemary and I went for a boat trip to the Scilly Isles with the two young men. It was quite rough but it didn't affect any of us. We stood on deck singing, 'We jolly sailor boys are up and aloft/And the land-lubbers lying down below, below'.

At the end of this lusty rendition, I spotted the Wolf Rock Lighthouse in the distance. Pointing to it, I cried, 'Look, the Wolf!' At this exact moment and in direct line with my finger, a man appeared at the top of the companionway (a naval term for staircase). We were both taken aback. I was embarrassed, he horrified, and the others burst out laughing – a man who chased women was termed a 'wolf' at the time. Nevertheless, we enjoyed a brief wander around St Mary's, a favourite haunt of Mary and Harold Wilson, quite unknown then but he was later to become the Labour Prime Minister.

Aumi was rather taken with me. On the boat the air was damp with sea spray and my hair, which had had a fairly successful bubble-cut with accompanying permanent wave, had suddenly formed into small curls all over. I was delighted; and my complexion – often marred by one spot or another appearing as soon as others disappeared, leaving pink scars behind which, as I mentioned earlier, I covered up with foundation (applied with a sponge) – looked wonderfully like alabaster. Aumi did have a 'wall eye', so perhaps his sight was a bit blurred, but all in all I was looking prettier than usual and took his eye – and Jack's as well! All these old expressions come flooding back. I don't talk this way any-more!

I preferred Aumi, although Jack did have incredibly large bright-blue eyes. Aumi and I talked a lot about acting and what we wanted to achieve in our lives. He was a Zionist and talked of going to a Kibbutz in Israel. He gave me the names of theatre agents in London, whom I could write to when I got home. They were not very illustrious ones, I'm afraid, but it gave a springboard to my thoughts of trying to become an actress after my amateur debut while I was in the WRNS. It was no surprise that I got no response when I contacted the agents. My sole experience had been one play, and I didn't know that I should have included a photograph of myself. But then I didn't have any – not proper studio portraits – just Mother's snaps with the Kodak and the ones caught on the prom by beach photographers.

I was in a quandary – if I had stayed on at school and passed my Higher School Certificate, the equivalent of A levels, I could have gone to university to study biology, which was the subject I'd been most interested in, as I explained earlier. I loved it, but I might not have got a grant from the local council. Now, having joined the WRNS straight from school, I was entitled to a government grant, but I hadn't taken my Higher School Certificate.

In the end, out of desperation, I applied for a job adver-tised in the *Evening Star*. The ad had been placed by a small electrical business in town that needed a cinema operator to show films to the German prisoners of war in their camps.

Thinking that I was at least qualified to do that, I applied for the post. In the end I was told that the owner of the business didn't think it was fair to the men who'd been locked away from women for several years to have a young, attractive woman suddenly appearing in their midst. It was very thoughtful of him, but unfortunate for me. He offered me the job of working in the office dealing with the film dispatch instead, as there was no one to do that either. He was a pleasant, friendly man, so I said, 'Yes, that would be lovely.' At least I would be earning some money.

I wasn't very good at working in an office; I've been a procrastinator since I was a young girl, always putting off till tomorrow what should have been done today. Mother's evaluation of me was 'June's a procrastinator' and 'June's very slow but she's very thorough'. These weren't helpful qualities in an office. Even in the WRNS, I would send the films back late! However, Mother would have been surprised to see how fast I was to become when I was dealing with five small children aged seven and under!

Chapter Fourteen

I was saved from my tedious office job by Rosebud – most likely just before I was sacked for incompetence. She came home from school one afternoon with an advertisement she'd found in *The Times* while in the school library. There was a new drama school starting in January 1947 called the Old Vic Theatre School; auditions were to be held in November. I applied and received the date for my audition and information about what would be required – I had to choose from one of four Shakespeare pieces, and bring another of my own choosing. I had no pieces of my own and wasn't particularly taken with the Shakespeare ones. I hadn't done any acting, apart from the play that I toured with in the WRNS. I was flummoxed, I rang the High School to ask if I could have a meeting with Miss Catley, my old English mistress.

Miss Catley adored the English language, poetry and plays; I think she was an 'actress manquée'. There was an air of dreaminess about her whenever she quoted from a poem. She suggested that I do the last speech of the Irish Queen in W. B. Yeats's poetic drama *Deirdre*, in which she lies beside Naoise in his coffin and intimates that she is going to kill herself so that she can be with her dead lover:

Now strike the wire, and sing to it a while,
Knowing that all is happy, and that you know
Within what bride-bed I shall lie this night,
And by what man, and lie close up to him,
For the bed's narrow . . .

As someone aspiring to be a dramatic actress, I had no interest in playing comedy: it was the perfect choice.

In late November, I took the train to London on what was to be a pivotal day in my life. I was ushered on to the stage by Pierre Lefèvre, a 30-year-old actor-turned-temporary-tutor, to be introduced to three men whose mission it was to open the school as part of the Old Vic Theatre Centre, where students were to be trained as actors, directors, theatre and costume designers and stage managers, feeding the Old Vic and the Young Vic Companies.

One of the three directors of this venture was Michel Saint-Denis, who brought his modified version of Stanislavski's training to the school. A Frenchman, he had already run a company in London during the Thirties called The Theatre Studio and had been the voice of the Free French,

Mother pregnant with me.

Mother shortly before being thrown through the windscreen of Father's open tourer due to him hitting a milestone while 'under the influence'.

Father – crouching – supervising painting of the garage, assisted by his staff: from left to right, Grandfather, a handyman, Uncle Eric, the gamekeeper (with broom), the gardener and the gardener's boy.

Me aged four months old in Mother's arms. She called me the jelly baby, always curled up. She didn't think I would ever walk, I was so soft.

Micie at twenty months old in the garden of 'The Hollies'.

Grandfather supporting me standing on his garden seat. I was about one year old.

Summer 1930. Me looking slightly stupid, baby Rosebud being held by Micie outside Father's greenhouse, where he grew his tomatoes at 50 Warwick Road.

Micie scratching her bottom to make me laugh.

Mother in a white-and-black polka dot semi-mourning dress, borrowed from Auntie Marie after the death of baby John Peter at sixteen days old the previous January. She wore it again after Micie's death two years later.

Our last holiday with Micie. I hadn't wet myself, my costume is wet in front because I'd sat at the water's edge and a wave had taken me by surprise.

Auntie Marie and Uncle Eric's wedding in 1935. Auntie's three cousins were bridesmaids – all called 'Louisa'. Mother – also a 'Louisa' – had made their dresses and hats. I am the youngest bridesmaid, aged eight. My green satin dress was bought for me, but Mother made my green net cap.

Auntie Marie and Uncle Eric's wedding reception at the scout hut on Spring Road. Mother and Father are at the front, Great Uncle Joe (Aunt Di's husband) is rear left, then Grandfather, Uncle Eric's brother and his numerous aunts.

Great Aunt Dolly (Monty's wife) and their daughter Sybil, who was also a cousin of Mother and Marie.

Rosebud and me, sitting on the running board of Uncle Eric's hand-painted car. Lois is in the driver's seat with Auntie Marie.

Uncle Eric outside the bungalow he built at weekends over a period of seven years, on his last motorbike, with a neighbour perched behind.

Me atop the air raid shelter with sister Rosebud and Yorkshire terrier Joey. Note my father's attempt to 'black out' the larder window. In summer the shelter assumed beauty when festooned with marrow plants. The photo was taken by Raoul, our Belgian refugee.

Uncle Eric (on the right) and best man Len, members of the Home Squad, with rifles at the ready – fit young men in reserved occupation, not a bit like *Dad's Army*!

Me, centre front, aged thirteen, with my 'monkey arms', between Cynthia Bowell and Barbara Robinson, fellow evacuees in Leicester. Behind is a disgraced soldier billeted next door.

Rosebud, aged thirteen, and me, aged sixteen, posing outside the French windows of 154 St John's Road.

Sub Lieutenant Colin Parsey and me walking on the prom at Troon (or was it Ayr?), where I had spent a weekend's leave from the Wrens.

With roommates in the lane between the Wrennery – 'Rosebank' in Queen Camel, Somerset – and the side door of the pub on our left, where I first got inebriated on 'scrumpy'.

Me in Somerset, in some sub lieutenant's car, just a few days after the end of the war. Colin had just been sent to the Far East.

On holiday in Penzance, having been de-mobbed. Still Mother's plump, jolly girl.

Mother and Father looking quite cheerful on a country drive in Suffolk.

Pea picking with students from the Old Vic School in Sandy, Bedfordshire.

The whole 'pea-picking ensemble'! I am third from the left, back row, and Donald – my beau – is crouching down in the centre.

Donald and myself at the Vic Wells Ball, in early 1948.

My untidy dressing room at the Old Vic School, which I shared with my best friend Doreen, and others.

Taken of me, aged twenty, by another student at the Old Vic flat.

My first husband, Johnny Garley, whom I met in the Old Vic Company in 1948 and married while we were both in the Young Vic Company on 24 February 1950.

Doreen, Joycie, Chrissie and me (standing), outside the scene dock door of the Old Vic Theatre on Waterloo Road. And Jack (bopping down), Chrissie's American friend from the Directors Course, in front.

With the Young Vic Company when it starts its provincial tour at the County Theatre, Bedford, on Monday, will be Mr. and Mrs. John Garley. Mr. Garley, whose mother resides in Kettering, is seen here with his wife, who plays under her maiden name of June Brown. (Story, Page Nine).

A press cutting from Kettering *Telegraph* newspaper.

While touring *The Knight of the Burning Pestle* in Holland with the Young Vic Company. Johnny, myself and Mrs Preston (a chaperone to her son, who was also in the cast) at Bloemendal. On the left is Michael Turner.

The Young Vic Company Tour on a boat to Holland, 1950.

Rosebud's wedding to Leighton at Kensington Register Office. Best man Dennis Spencer is on the left. Rosebud had borrowed my suit only hours before, which I had been wearing under my red gabardine coat. I was a little chilly in the January air!

Johnny, in character make-up and wig, and me in *Measure for Measure* at Stratford-upon-Avon. I had just finished doing his eye make-up for him, which he relied on me to do.

The Emmanuel Street Story, The Embassy Theatre 1952, playing the young Jewish girl.

Measure For Measure, The Shakespeare Memorial Theatre 1955.

Playing Lady Macbeth at The Birmingham Repertory Theatre 1957, the sleep-walking scene with John Carlin and Sonia Fraser.

broadcasting to France during the war, using the nom-de-plume Jacques Duchesne.

He had introduced Churchill's famous broadcast to the French after the fall of France in 1940. There was only one chair in front of the microphone, and it was Michel who was sitting in it when Churchill entered the studio. He asked, 'Where shall I sit?'

Michel went to rise. Churchill stopped him with, 'No, you must introduce me. I shall sit on your knee.' Which he duly did.

According to Michel, Churchill was very emotional during his speech, tears were streaming down his face as he spoke, in his execrable French: ' ...We shall defend our island, whatever the cost may be. We shall fight on the beaches, we shall fight on the landing grounds, we shall fight in the fields and in the streets, we shall fight in the hills; we shall never surrender ...' Churchill loved France and admired the French and he was distraught that they had surrendered, but France was being attacked on two sides, by the Germans in the north and the Italians from the south; and also, they did not want their beautiful capital city of Paris destroyed in the fighting that would have ensued.

Anyway, at the audition Glen Byam Shaw was another of the directors, and he was mainly responsible for the acting. He had been a West End actor and then a successful West End director. He had directed the first production of *The Winslow Boy*, in which his wife Angela Baddeley played the leading part of the boy's sister. She was to become well known in her late days as Mrs Bridges, the cook in *Upstairs, Downstairs*.

I once asked Glen why he had given up acting. He loved rehearsing, he told me, but hated performing. I was his opposite; I lacked confidence in rehearsals – shy of showing what I wanted to do – and felt more freedom in performing. I came to enjoy both processes equally – I gained my confidence, I suppose.

The last of the three was George Devine, who dealt with the administrative side of running the school, but his forte was comedy – he took our comedy improvisation classes and directed our comedy scenes. He was an extremely good comedy actor himself. If I could draw a cartoon of him it would be of a weighty man with thick unkempt dark hair, piercing brown eyes – he was of Greek extraction, so I was told – smoking a filthy old pipe, a doughnut in one hand and scratching his bottom with the other. He was to be the most successful of them all, nine years later as the overall director of the renaissance of the Royal Court Theatre in Sloane Square in London, bringing the first of what became known as the 'kitchen sink' dramas to the stage, with *Look Back In Anger* by John Osborne.

Pierre read in for my audition, and I started it off with my awful rendition of Mistress Quickly – to me, a very nondescript piece of prose. I performed it – if it could be called that – with no sense of the comedy. I don't think it created a very good impression. Then came *Deirdre* – it was a very short soliloquy, so I didn't require Pierre's assistance. Something happened: I was suddenly caught up in the feeling of it and the beauty of the poetry, something I had not felt when rehearsing on my own.

Finally, I was asked to do an improvisation. 'We'd like you

to improvise being in a country lane when an enemy plane flies overhead,' someone shouted from out front. I was dumbfounded. I had never heard of improvisation. I couldn't run up a flight of steps, as I had done in real life – there weren't any to hand and I was in my new – bought for the occasion, first time of wearing – tomato-red, fine wool, straight-skirted knee-length dress and my new high-heeled black suede shoes. I wasn't dressed for the part! I made the best of it – tottered across the stage, looked up, flung myself face down on the far-from-pristine stage, got up and promptly dusted myself down!

I was asked to go down into the auditorium. The first question I was asked came from Glen – Mr Byam Shaw, as I addressed him in the early days:

'Why did you choose Mistress Quickly?'

That was easy to answer. 'Because I didn't like any of the others.'

I was asked how I would be funded if I were accepted.

'By a government grant from having been in the W.R.N.,' I explained. 'But I'd need to know soon as I would have to apply quickly?'

They told me that I would be given a place, and straight away I burst into tears. In my youth, I cried at the drop of a hat – when I was filled with joy or with desolation. I wish I could still be so spontaneous now: to go from the heights to the depths with an open heart. I travel in a flatter land now – a few little hills and dales. I must have worn myself out with all those emotions.

Back home in Ipswich I explained to my boss that I would be leaving at Christmas because I was going to drama school.

He was delighted for me, he said, and more probably for himself as he had been spared the task of sacking me for the inadequacy of my clerical duties!

I was able to be happy that Christmas, filled with the expectation of what was to come.

Chapter Fifteen

On our first day at the new drama school we were given our practice costumes, which we were to wear every day. They consisted of a navy wool sleeveless top with a round neck, a pair of pants that covered the tops of our thighs, and a full-length skirt which was in two pieces. Mine was blue wool and quite warm. Some were a rather thin black material, so I was fortunate as that winter was so cold. The skirt had poppers down one side so you could have either a simple A-line skirt, or join the two parts together with the poppers to make a full skirt drawn in at the waist with a cord for period parts. We also had flat black pumps, like Greek dancing shoes.

The next day was the official opening of the school. There were about fifteen guests, and the press took photographs. Glen Byam Shaw opened the proceedings saying we were now actors – not chosen half for our talent, half to pay the fees. He was sure we could all become professionals and we would be treated as such. We must never be late, never slacken, must be able to work on our own and at the same time be light-hearted and gay. Actors are simple at heart. All truth is.

We were told the history of the formation of the Theatre Centre, of which we were a part. He told us that he wanted to create one theatre to cater for young people, and one to try out new plays and classics. We were the first students of a brand-new venture. He was not there just as the director, but also as a friend. There were opening speeches from Ellen Wilkinson, Minister of Education; Laurence Olivier; Michel Saint-Denis; and the Chairman of the Arts Council, Ernest Pooley.

Olivier spoke next about acting and how we should grow like a tree – we were young trees with branches all over and we must not turn into just one branch. You watch a tree grow steadily and evenly. Grow the roots firmly in truth and belief; it is truth and belief that matter. And we were going to learn how to present reality.

So training began – it was based on Stanislavski but modernised by Michel Saint-Denis. We were split into four sections and I was put into section one. There were thirty students altogether. We had classes in voice, singing, movement, gymnastics, fencing and the history of the theatre.

Litz Pisk took us for movement; she must have been in her fifties but she was so supple. She always wore black – a long black skirt that she'd lift the hem of in front and tuck it into her waistband so they looked like a pair of Turkish trousers. The hardest exercise was one where she showed us how to flex our knees, keeping our back completely straight until the hands could touch the floor in front and then behind. Unless you're very young and supple you won't find it possible. We achieved it after a struggle. It was impossible!

Jani Strasser, an Austrian, who had been the singing coach for the Glyndebourne Opera Company, taught us voice production. This involved what he called the 'fish's gills'. He was a very enthusiastic, lively man and a great source of encouragement.

He would teach us a way of breathing that wasn't just about the diaphragm – he said we had to use the base of our backs, as if a lavatory being flushed from a cistern, the water going down into the bowl and suddenly flushing up on each side. We developed such strong voices. I wish I still had mine; I've smoked too much and not breathed enough – too much television work, not enough acting in large theatres.

I demonstrated the fish's gills to Terry Wogan once, when I appeared as his guest. I never really knew what I was going to say on talk shows and just hoped I would go off at a tangent that was entertaining. Terry was lovely: he gave me the floor and I enlisted his help demonstrating ... And here's a funny thing – to quote Max Miller – when I was in hospital, having given birth to my first child, I did my ballet exercises every day at the end of my bed. A week later when I left the hospital, my waist had reduced to twenty-four inches. Ironic, given how much I shunned exercise as a young girl – and how little I do now!

Someone in Ipswich had recommended I stay with some people they knew in Edith Road. I travelled up to London for that first term at drama school, and I had moved in with

Phyllis, who had been a Tiller Girl. Her husband started asking me out with him in the evenings, which I didn't care for, and Phyllis seemed to be intimidated by him. So, unwilling I'd go to small clubs with him around Kensington. We hardly spoke, I felt he used me as 'arm candy', which made me uncomfortable. So very quickly, I found myself a room at the back of Earl's Court Station.

That winter of 1947 was terrible. We were based temporarily at the Froebel Institute in Colet Gardens, Baron's Court.

I remember that the snow was two or three feet deep and it was extremely difficult to get fuel; the Froebel Institute wasn't heated at all, it was absolutely freezing. The way we got warm in Litz Pisk's movement classes was to lie on the cold wooden floor in our gym costumes – those bottoms in itchy navy-blue wool – and imagine that we were lying under a hot sun on a beach – it worked! The only other time we were warm was when we sat in front of our gas fires in our bedsitting-rooms; it really was a terrible, terrible winter. I still managed to get to school on the Tube however, in spite of the heavy snow; there was never any trouble, and even the buses ran.

One of the students, her name was Ann, had to leave the school in the middle of that first term as the directors discovered that she suffered from epilepsy. I remember her running out of the school on the morning she was told, in her long rehearsal skirt, out into the street. She went through those high drifts of snow, with no coat and I remember her coming back later, her heavy wool skirt sodden and clinging to her legs. Poor Ann, she was distraught. I was so sorry for her that I asked her to come and live with me. It was a very unhappy period, she drifted around Earls Court finding friends amongst the students from LAMDA (London Academy of Music and Dramatic Art) in the Cromwell Road, and in the evenings I would tell her what we had been doing that day in an attempt to help her continue with the training.

The worst moment during the time we lived together came when she asked me to describe exactly what happened to her during one of these fits. She had consulted a hospital in her search for a way to permit her to return to the Vic School – she desperately wanted to act – and they'd asked for this information. I knew I had to tell her the truth, but it was very hard for me to do so; she had no idea of the indignity she suffered. I'd found that putting a cold wet flannel on her forehead at least prevented the headaches that normally followed, but I lived in constant apprehension. I didn't realise how much it was affecting me until one night, asleep in my bed, I sat bolt upright as the door opened, instantly awake and fearful, and it was only Ann coming home late. We lost touch when we both went home for the summer holidays and I have often wondered what happened to her.

During this first term we were doing scenes from *Antony and Cleopatra,* and as an enormous treat we were allowed to go to the Piccadilly Theatre, where Edith Evans was playing Cleopatra. Godfrey Tearle was Antony and Anthony Quayle was a wonderful Enobarbus, and we were to enact our scenes on the actual stage set for the London production. The play was being directed by Glen Byam Shaw, our director at the school, who had also been directing our scenes. It was a most

humiliating experience, in a way. I was doing a scene from
Antony and Cleopatra, and to actually sit on the throne that
Edith Evans sat on as Cleopatra every night was amazing
because it seemed so big that one didn't seem to fill it. I
mean, I wasn't a skinny little person, but I just felt that I
hadn't the stature to fill that stage – which of course none of
us had. We weren't experienced actresses. That was the great
thing about the West End actors, their enormous stature. It
didn't matter how small or slim they were, they had this
tremendous aura around them.

Donald had a strong Edinburgh accent which worked
against him at school. I watched him playing Antony in
Antony and Cleopatra in that first term and I only remember
'Nay, nay, Octavia not only that' which made me laugh
inside. It was a shame that he couldn't rid himself of his
accent as it did not become 'fashionable' until Peter O'Toole
and Albert Finney's era in the Sixties, when the Queen's
English was no longer necessary whatever you played, prince
or pauper.

Donald and I became friendly and he started also being
friendly with another student, Christine Hearne, a Man-
cunian of Irish forbears, and Shaun O'Riordan (who became
a producer of the Charlie Drake shows, who wasn't easy to
work with, so I heard), who said laughingly to me, you only
go out with Christine to make sure she isn't with Donald! Oh
the subterfuge, and he was right. Christine Hearne later
became one of my dear friends.

So, any old road, as they say in Suffolk, Donald and I did
become lovers (start counting) for all the rest of our time at
the school.

I remember standing on the stage on a much later occasion when I was understudying one of the women in *Much Ado About Nothing*, and I was next to Peggy Ashcroft. I felt I couldn't get too close to her because she too had this aura around her, a field of energy, and you had to stand at least two feet away to accommodate the size of it. It was the same with Alec Guinness. I was once called for an audition for a play that he was doing and he very kindly read with me. But by this time I hadn't the voice I'd had when I was a student because I'd done so much 'little' theatre – we didn't call it 'fringe' in those days, we used to call the theatres around London 'little'. I'd done so many of those, in which the power of your voice wasn't required, that it had lost its power. I remember being amazed at the resonance and power of Alec Guinness's voice. I realised it was practice that was necessary, but if you weren't given the opportunity it was impossible to accomplish.

While we were at the Piccadilly Theatre, our section and section four did our scenes while the other sections watched. Michel Saint-Denis, Glen Byam Shaw and George Devine and all the staff were there. They felt it was flat, though they said section four were very good.

I was pleased with the way Doreen had worked, and I was also pleased with the way she'd worked on the scene when she had nothing to say! In fact, when she had nothing to say she was better! He said Doreen had, to a certain extent, found the continuity of the line/life; but her 'carriage bracket', or shoulders, were small and cramped and her voice was not good, her vowels were tight and she fixed her words too soon! She was very good when she wasn't saying anything. Doreen's response was that she 'felt much happier about it'! So he found a little bit of praise to offer that was quite unusual.

Sadly she died last year. I managed to get to Bournemouth to see her in hospital after a major stroke. She lay there with a peaceful happy face. I sat and talked to her and suddenly her face seemed to tense in irritation. I was holding her hand, our elbows together on the bed. 'I'm sorry Dor,' I said, 'I won't bring you back', and her face softened and she pulled my arm sharply, strongly to her shoulder.

I spoke at her funeral a week later to speak of her as 'a friend', saying how true a one, she was always happy for you, sympathetic towards you, understanding, generous. There were no negatives, she was a precious friend and I would miss her very much. As I do. I realise now that she was the friend to me that Micie was.

I remember reading a few palms one day in the canteen and Doreen told me five years ago what I'd said for her 52 years later.

1) An affair at twenty-five that will come to nothing. Her comment: 'No comment.'
2) A big change at thirty. Her comment: 'Very true.'
3) Happy marriage with three children: Her comment, 'Sort of right, one miscarriage and two adopted.'
4) One of whom will be famous. Her comment: 'Still waiting.'

As Doreen's diary outlined 'we were not chosen for dramatic schools. They were sure we could become actors and actresses.

We had the ability. So we must be treated as actors. Discipline would be strict. We must never be late, there is no excuse. An actor cannot hold up the curtain. He must be punctual at rehearsals. We must enjoy our work, be light-hearted and gay. Actors are simple at heart. All truth is'. I learned so much that term, Doreen quotes some of Laurence Olivier's speech to us, that acting was 'like a tree. We were young trees with fresh buds shooting out all over it. We might develop one branch more than another. But we were to be careful of devoting all our attention to one branch of acting as we may then be unable to turn to the other branches.' But for me the bit that always stands out was his warning 'We must be careful not to let our ambition outgrow our ability'.

It all sounds terribly serious but there were lighter times too – I celebrated my twentieth birthday by giving a fancy-dress party on 16 February in my room in Earl's Court. I invited the students from my group and a few others. We were about ten in all. I wore my white lace top from the evening dress that I'd bought with my £20 gratuity given to me on my demob from the WRNS, my navy knicker bottoms from the gym costume provided by the school, stockings and high heels and transformed myself into a principal boy. I think now I was a bit of a show-off but I had nothing else to concoct myself a costume with. The party was very slow getting off the ground. I remember saying to Doreen 'This isn't working is it?' We had no alcohol; most of us didn't drink it very much so there was nothing to oil our wheels. Just as it was warming up the landlady knocked on the door and asked us to make less noise. I didn't even think we had music playing; I didn't even own a radio. That put a damper on it. We didn't know each other very well, there was silence and embarrassment until Norman Ayrton came to the rescue by proving himself a great raconteur, telling us his stories and jokes to muted laughter for over an hour and a half, then people started drifting home. I was very grateful to Norman, as I'd thought it was going to be a fiasco.

At school we'd been rehearsing our scenes from *Anthony and Cleopatra* and two days after this party we went to Piccadilly Theatre to perform them on the set of the London production starring Dame Edith Evans and Godfrey Teasle. We had seen their performance on complimentary tickets. Although Dame Edith sounded lovely she was twenty years too old and had very little passion nor emotional feeling in her portrayal. Anthony Quayle was an excellent Enobarbus and Godfrey Tearle gave his good solid performance. However, this was a daunting experience for us . . .

We had our criticisms afterwards from Michel, Glen and George.

I couldn't have been too dreadful or I'd have remembered what they said to me but I don't, so that's a relief.

The first term finished on 2 April with a school dance. I stayed to the end mostly in the company of Donald and then together we walked to the Lyons Corner House at Charing Cross and had a very early breakfast. I arrived back at my room at 3.30 a.m. to find Doreen there. She'd missed her last train and was dossing down on the floor. Poor Anne, who couldn't go to the party, had kept her talking until then. It would be 4.30 a.m. before we got to sleep.

During the Easter break, I went with Doreen to Stratford-upon-Avon to see some Shakespeare plays. Donald and

Edgar Wreford were to join us. I had stayed the weekend at Doreen's home and her father had taken us to London, and to Scotts for lunch, before taking us to catch the train. That was where we were supposed to meet the chaps. We missed them somehow and arrived at our lodging house at two minutes to seven to find a note from them to say meet us at the theatre at seven o'clock. We rushed there and there was no sign of them. Finally Doreen and I went in to see the play at the end of the second act to find they'd been sitting comfortably inside throughout.

The other three had received letters already from the school confirming that they had passed the probationary term. I had heard nothing and was worried that I might have been thrown out after the first term. Doreen and I went to see *Dr Faustus*, which we enjoyed. We had a lovely walk along the river and met John Blatchley, introduced ourselves and he asked us to tea the following day. It transpired that he was very enthusiastic about the Old Vic school but didn't have much time for the Stratford company. Talking at length about criticism and the difficulties of working in the professional theatre, he said that he hated his part in *Measure for Measure*. We went to see *Measure for Measure* in the evening and would see why he 'didn't like the production and thought it was very badly cast'. I remember that he wore a black hat and carried a walking stick – very much the 'actor-laddie'.

We decided to give the theatre a miss the next night and went to see that wonderful film *Odd Man Out* starring James Mason, who was excellent and surrounded by a brilliant cast of Irish actors; a much-praised film.

I'd heard nothing from the Vic School by the time we left Stratford. I was so concerned that I phoned Glen, having found his number in the directory. Glen answered the phone and I could hardly speak, my voice was so shaky. He said 'You silly girl, of course you've passed', but in a very kind way. I phoned Doreen immediately and then I left for home. It turned out that my letter from the school was there.

I came back to London with Rosebud, who was going to the Royal College of Music to study piano and voice. She switched later, taking voice as a major subject. I had found us a room with a double bed. Stupid idea as it couldn't have passed as a bed-sitting room; it was all bed! It was a rather grotty room near Earl's Court Exhibition Centre. The first night there we put the light out and very soon Rosebud began to complain that the bed was itchy. I switched the light on, took one look at Rosebud's side of the bed and in a staccato voice a deep sound came out of me – 'Get-out-of-that-bed'. She leapt out in fright. I had seen a stream of brown, spade-like beetles moving down her side of the bed. They were bedbugs. I had never seen one before but I knew instantly what they were. I grabbed a small bottle of iodine, emptied it into the basin and scooped up one as evidence. In my youth I'd been a Girl Guide, their motto, 'Be prepared'. We took off our nighties, shook them frantically to rid ourselves of a stray bug and jumped up and down, packed everything we owned into Father's trunk and walked in the night from the back of Earl's Court tube station to Notting Hill, where my friend William Reid, a Scottish painter who was on the design course at the school, lived.

We woke him up and he let us sleep on the dining-room floor. It was a large house but he wasn't prepared for visitors.

I'd met Willie at a performance of a ballet, maybe one of Margot Fonteyn's performances, a brilliant dancer, full of passion and perfect line and balance. I saw her in *Sleeping Beauty* with her four suitors before her, she stood on one point, raised her arm and brought it down gently, slowly on to one of their hands, one after the other. I never saw any other ballerina take such time, stay poised on that one point for so long. I loved her. Willie was attracted to me when I smiled at him with my eyes as well as my mouth, he told me.

The next morning Rosebud, covered with swollen bites, had her first day at the Royal College, she had never suffered from spots as I had but had to suffer the temporary embarrassment on this occasion. I left to find a lodging place and by some good fortune found two rooms normally used by two students from the school which they had kept on for the Easter holiday. Rosebud and I moved in, but not before we lugged Father's solid leather trunk down the stairs to the street. We carried it between us to a road halfway up to the vicarage off Kensington Church Street.

I armed myself with a DDT spray which I used in the house in case we'd brought a bug with us and I washed every scrap of our clothing by hand.

Then I returned to normal life – a student at the school, and included Rosebud in my social life. We went everywhere; to the ballet, the theatre poetry readings. We were avid to learn. Whole groups of us would go together. On the 27 April Doreen, me, Rosebud, Ann (Morrish), Donald, Edgar, Shaun O'Riordan, Margaret, Sheila Lader, Mary, Lesley

(Retey) and Norman went to the Apollo Society reading at the Globe Theatre. Michel Saint-Denis, Margaret Rawlings and Robert Speight read poems.

At school we were doing character improvisation if I remember. I found clothes and created a pregnant woman. Why? It was my fear not my hope. A subconscious foretelling of what was to come ten years later.

James Forsyth attended these improvisation classes meaning to write scenarios from them. He was not aware of me then and wrote nothing for me. The next year he was to write *Penthesilea* and fall in love with me. Appearances, appearances, do not trust them!

Lessons and lectures went on as usual. In the first term we'd had a group voice showing with Jani. We did the same again in the second term. Glen was angry with me for showing off. I was deeply upset, Litz found me weeping on the stairs. 'I wasn't,' I sobbed, 'I just was trying to do it well!'

Powys Thomas, who later married Ann Morrish, a beautiful clever student with a wonderful nature, took me to his room and put me into a state of hypnosis and calmed me down. That evening there was to be a showing of scenes for *The Cherry Orchard*. My part was a girl who was a show-off, Dunyasha, a lady's maid who has ideas above her station.

Glen complimented me on being able to do it with confidence after having been brought low by his criticism of me for the self-same failing. The praise should have been given to Powys.

How often people get the wrong interpretation. I was doing a mimed scene of a sad child looking wistfully around her. She was seen as a sulky child – I could not have been doing it well, obviously.

In July of that year, a lot of us moved the school to the Old Vic Theatre in the Waterloo Road on the backs of lorries. Imagine an historic theatre is your school with its hallowed stage and auditorium. The downstairs bar was our canteen, the actors' dressing rooms were our dressing rooms. We weren't supposed to go up into the gods, they weren't safe after the London bombings, but we did sneak up there of course. That was a heavenly time in my life.

Chapter Sixteen

The second year of the school started in September and we were now installed in the Old Vic Theatre, where I transferred my food rationing book to David Greig, the big grocery store that used to be next to the stage door. We felt as if we were proper actors.

I was happy with Donald and to be in a proper dressing room with Doreen and Joanna Korwin (now Anna Korwin), a refugee from Poland who I'm still in contact with today – it was a foretaste of the future.

Last term I'd been staying at the Theatre Girls Club in Greek Street W1 with Sheila Lader; very convenient to Waterloo and very cheap, £1.50 a week, for a cubicle, breakfast and supper.

Miss Bell managed the club and she enjoyed Sheila and me being there as we were theatre and not variety.

After a few weeks we were given a large room at the top of the building opposite the laundry room and she gave me a pair of long white evening gloves which I still possess. Going to our room one day I reached the top landing and exclaimed, 'Oh! What a lovely smell of violets.' The cleaning lady happened to be coming out of the laundry room, 'It's the floor polish,' she said hastily. I've heard of Ronuk, which smelt of ordinary floor polish and lavender but never before or since have I heard of one smelling of violets. Since then I have often smelt violets or my mother's face powder. That and premonitions are my only other psychic gifts.

I left Greek Street as Chrissie and Joycie Ash had just moved into a flat, 102d New Bond Street, which belonged to Chattie Salaman. She was the wife of John Blatchley, who was an assistant tutor at the school. She was the sister of Merula, Alec Guinness's wife. Chrissie asked me if I'd like to join them at Bond Street. I felt privileged and accepted immediately.

I moved into the flat – two rooms with kitchen and bathroom. No carpet on the floor, just a few thin rugs, a double bed, single bed, a dining table and chairs – sparsely furnished but we loved what became known as 'the Bond Street flat'. It became the meeting place for all the students who dropped in when they passed by.

Chrissie, Joycie and I took turns in the beds, so to speak. First, your place was the right side of the double for a week, then the left side and, great treat, the single bed. There were usually students on the floor, Doreen often amongst them. I had said that I would sell Doreen for thirty bob (£1.50p) my red suit that I'd had to lend her when her coat was stolen at our end of term party – there she was in her practice costume, so I said, 'Come and sleep at the flat and I'll lend you my red suit for tomorrow.'

She looked jolly good in it.

We all talked, smoked, drank endless cups of tea together with toast made in front of the gas fire. The rent was 4 guineas a week (£4.20) and we paid 35 pence each to cover the gas and electricity bills for the week.

At school we were starting rehearsals for the plays for the school shows. I had been given the wonderful part of Penthesilea, the Amazon Queen in a play of that name specially written for us by James Forsyth. What long rehearsals we had; it wasn't going to be performed till May of the next term, and this was 22 January.

During the rehearsals, we were continuing with our classes. In voice, movement, acrobatics. One of our stunts was to jump from an eight or nine foot high ledge on to the mat below. I jumped, 'Well done,' said Mr Alexander. I got up and hobbled off with a sprained ankle.

We used masks with white papier faces with holes cut in the eye sockets. The idea of them was to make our bodies express what our faces were cut off from showing. It was fascinating to work with them and strange how different the same masks looked on different people, as if the character of the face behind it showed through.

The play *Penthesilea* includes a poem which describes an orgasm. Here it is:

The end of roses is their scent
It is in Artemis' intent

That woman like the rose
Should grown from bud to bloom
And not fade there
It is in Artemis' intent
That woman know the sweet despair
For which the petal
All are spent
When a moment the full soul ascends
The body like a stair
And hovers like the perfume where
Artemis rested from the hunt.

I had to interpret this poem for the others in my dressing room as they didn't understand it. The poem has to rise in from 'the full soul ascends' in one breath with no pauses or full stops and a dying fall from 'hovers' on downwards. I have a love of words so it was marvellous for me to have this opportunity.

Three weeks later into the term I would have my twenty-first birthday party. Everyone was invited and they all came. Doreen says there was lovely food but I don't remember it. Before it started I was very upset because Donald had rung to say he wouldn't be there. I, in floods of tears, flung myself on the bed and implored the girls to make him come.

'Make him come. Make him come!' I kept repeating. They did my bidding! So I had a wonderful birthday, as I had at Shaun O'Riordan's party, but in quite a different way.

Shaun's father, who lived in Sri Lanka (then called Ceylon), had sent him money to take his girlfriend, Tarn Bassett, out to dinner. Was it the Bagatelle or the original Mirabelle? One or the other. They were two of the most exclusive restaurants in London. Shaun invited me as our twenty-first birthdays were very close together, two days apart I think. Donald was invited to come with me. That was an unusual and delightful treat.

Rehearsals for *Penthesilea,* the school show, were heavy; Donald and I were in different plays so we didn't see much of each other and I was worried about my performance and having difficulty with laughing at a very important moment. Fortunately Michel took over the direction from Suria Magito, another one of our tutors. I couldn't laugh when Penthesilea felled Apollo, standing looking down at him lying on the ground at her feet. It was supposed to be a triumphant sound and nothing emerged from my mouth. Nothing. I couldn't do it. Then Michel came upon the scene and there was a sea-change.

'Just make a noise, ha ha ha ha, he he he he, ho ho ho ho.'

He looked and sounded so ridiculous that he gave me courage to make a fool of myself – two or three strangled noises. In the end that laugh came easily and Peter Copley, after the performance he'd seen, said, 'I'll never forget your laugh.'

The lesson being to dare, to dare to make a fool of yourself. Do it!

Donald had begun to seem a little remote. I remember very clearly the moment he told me he thought we should end our affair. We were on the Embankment of the Thames and I was turned away from him looking down the river and he said, 'You see, you don't care.'

I turned my head and looked at him, tears were streaming down my face. I wasn't acting but it was rather a dramatic moment. We didn't split up.

I thought he was overshadowed by Powys, who was playing Apollo opposite my Penthesilea. In all honesty, Donald was a better actor but he had not lost his Scottish accent and he hadn't an ear for a tune; I think that Powys being favoured affected him a great deal.

So life still went on as normal. In the evenings and at weekends we still went around in groups. I remember one Sunday going for a walk in Epping Forest – walk and talk was satisfying entertainment – and then a cheap Chinese meal, only found in Limehouse, the Chinese quarter, which we found interesting. Then back to the Bond Street flat to talk about acting and the theatre.

Six of us, including Rosebud, went to see the Stratford-upon-Avon production of *Romeo and Juliet* that had been brought to London. Laurence Payne, who was playing Romeo, was ill and the understudy was on. He was marvellous, much better than his principal whom we'd seen before on our Stratford trip. I'm sure he was Sir Donald Sinden.

We saw the first production of Benjamin Britten's *Albert Herring*. There were eight of us. Very disappointed in the music we were, but we found the opera quite funny. Lovely moments and bad ones, we agreed from our high position as students!

Two nights later fifteen of us went to see *The Rape of Lucrece*, which we enjoyed more than *Albert Herring*. Donald didn't care much for the opera, particularly the Avant Garde. He never came to the operas with us.

Suddenly the performances of the school shows were upon us. Donald and I had not seen much of each other. We had two separate shows with four performances of show A and four of show B. We were all in a state of nervous tension. Show A gave their performances first of *The Wedding*, by Chekov, *Our Town*, by Thornton Wilder and a medley of songs, *The Carnivale*, in which we all sang.

On the 30 May we had the first night of Show B – *Penthesilea*. It was a tremendous success, we received a standing ovation and we had very good notices. I was very upset by the headline in *The News Chronicle*. We were doing group theatre, we shouldn't have headlines like 'Old Vic Finds a Young Star', and nobody should be singled out! How innocent I was.

That notice did me great harm. Going into the stage door I met Michel and he greeted me with, 'Ah de yoong star but ken yoo do it again?'

Something I hadn't questioned.

Immediately I thought, 'What if I can't?'

The stage felt cold, dead to me as I went on that night, and so was my performance. If he meant to spur me on, he'd chosen the wrong person. The third night was better and the last better still but neither of them came up to that first night.

But after the first night of *Letters Home* at the New End Theatre in Hampstead, thirty years later, I answered his question. Anna Nigh and I received fantastic notices for our respective parts of Sylvia and her mother Aurelia Plath. I thought, 'They're coming to see me, what if I fail?'

I spoke out loud to myself: 'Don't be such a fool June, you can do it again and again and again.'

And I did.

Two years after Michel's remark, it came to me that it had done me a lot of damage, despite him not intending it; he caused me to doubt myself for thirty years and stopped me perhaps from achieving what I might have done.

A few weeks after the school show, at the end of our training, Donald didn't appear. The last time we spoke he had been talking to me intently and rather strangely about spiritual matters and I was concerned about him.

Suddenly he didn't turn up at the Old Vic School, I was very worried about him and I borrowed the keys to his flat from Richard Burrell, his flatmate, and went to Addison Gardens in West London. I opened the door and the room was in darkness. I switched the light on to find Donald standing stock still in the middle of the room.

I went up to him, took hold of him said, 'What are you doing?' and shook him. He didn't answer me, I couldn't get him to speak, I left him and went back to the school, straight to Glen Byam Shaw.

'You must do something about Donald, Glen!'

He looked at me, 'Oh those big tears,' taking out his handkerchief.

He contacted Mrs MacRae, she and Donald's elder brother Ian came from Edinburgh to take him back with them to a psychiatric hospital.

Donald would have been going to the Old Vic Company

with me – it was heart-breaking that he should suffer the burden of schizophrenia.

During the rehearsals for *Twelfth Night* in London I visited Donald in the Edinburgh psychiatric hospital. I walked through several locked doors before reaching him. When he saw me his face lit up, then fell into a blankness.

I'd stayed at the Donmaree with Marie, Donald's mother, and Ian. I knew now why she'd been so anxious for me to marry Donald, buying me the brown silk dress with painted flowers from Harrods and saying she was going to buy Donald a tartan dress kilt for the wedding – she was hoping it would save him from more bouts of schizophrenia. It had happened once before; he had been very distressed at the age of seventeen-and-a-half that his father, a man who had been a captain in the Merchant Navy, would not return to sea at the outbreak of war. He was, himself, awaiting his call-up into the Royal Air Force; it came too late, he was found in Edinburgh walking the streets in an Air Force Officer's uniform to which he was not entitled. When he came out he joined the Merchant Navy.

I don't know what Donald experienced during the war years, nobody talked about it, like Raoul and his escape via the Dunkirk beaches and Ernie Page, a boy I knew of my age who was in the Merchant Navy. Each of the ships Ernie served on being torpedoed and three times rescued from the waters of the Atlantic Ocean. An eighteen year old who never told me more than I've just told you. He, after the war, went into a psychiatric hospital.

After a year a small Young Vic company had been formed

and Donald had been given some parts in it. I remained part of the main Young Vic company.

I met Donald again on a railway platform during the tour, by which time I was married to Johnny. Donald was plump and jolly, the result of his electric shock treatment I believe. He was a man I didn't recognise, he told me I needed someone who was light-hearted and humorous, but Johnny had darkness in him which I was yet to discover.

Back in London I bumped into James Forsyth outside the stage door. Ralph Richardson called him 'Our tame playwright'. He was attached to the company as a writer, although nothing came of it for him. He handed me an envelope and asked if I would meet him in a basement café an old-fashioned tea room on the Charing Cross Road. I thought it was money maybe, which would have been very welcome, but it was a poem.

> *God knows there is no need to see*
> *Fate in operation to explain*
> *Why I should meet your eyes once in a day*
> *And have no rest*
> *For sleep defeats my mocking*
> *And the dream gives me away*
> *It's ludicrous my love but it is so*
> *That I against experience should grow*
> *Childish in duty*
> *Yet nothing needs surprise me now that you have reached*
> *   your beauty*

Thank you for that achievement
And it's grace
And if my words inhabiting your mind
Have left some favourite meaning on your face
Can I be blamed if tenderly I trace
Those 'seeds of meaning'
Not now in the wind
But brought to bear where most I find satisfaction
Further than this
I will not go
For I've no right
But I would have you know
That you are loved
For it would be
A miserliness in me
To hoard the proof
Of what you seem to see
Yet fear unproved.
Take it dear as additional riches to life
It cannot be 'part of the battle, part of the strife, there is no
    hunt, no quarry' here to persue
The end for me is in the hope that you may use
The tenderness in this
To grow greater in your art
Your heart will know no hurt from me
More than it has
Which this may part allay.

James Law Forsyth 1948

In this poem I have underlined where he was quoting from his play *Penthesilea*. He was seeing me as his creation rather than me as an actress.

Below, in comparison, is the poem he wrote for my character in *Penthesilea* in January 1948:

I do not come from pillared cities in the plain
Where words like weapons from the brain
May strike like arrows where they aim
I come from where the winds may blow
A seed of meaning from the woods below
Which is not accurate and yet
May go straight to the heart
But this I know for all the years
That I have called my longing to the hills
There has been no echo until now
And I know now it is the voice of love.

All I had done was put my arm around him for a photograph and he thought I was in love with him!

Poor deluded man, his wife was pregnant with his second son.

I became obsessed with his plays. I was to discover the rhythm of them. I remember having tea with him one day, probably in the same basement tea room.

'It's like a heart, a dynamo. It beats Jamie, it beats.'

And so it did. He was so pleased, delighted that I had found the key to the way he wrote. We were to become very close for a while.

Then there was the day that we made love. The experience left me utterly cold; it was as if a feather was touching me. I refused further encounters and James reviled me in a letter as being shallow. I couldn't tell him that if I continued with this illicit, unsatisfactory affair I would have felt as if I were a prostitute. I think I have his letter still! He also wrote another poem for me:

She who holds all my hopes of peace
Seeks her peace with strangers,
She who is the answer to the question at my breast
Roves about the world and without rest
Questions those who do not care to know
The nature of the answers.
Must she go drifting past and I, like a ghost,
Cry warning in a word that always dies
Short of her senses.
Will this seeking only lead to me
When tired beyond the hopes of peace
I lie in a dry armistice with love?
Will sorrow bracket time to make the stairway that we
    seemed to climb
Towards a common sky?
Or will it be evening when she sees the view
I see all day spread before us
Oh, why should she who holds all my hopes of peace

Seek her peace with strangers
And increase the number of her failures
And my dangers from the thousand little deaths

James Law Forsyth 1948

I met him many years later and did poetry readings for him. I bought five of his watercolours and told him delicately what my feelings had been, and he seemed to understand. By this time his second wife Ann had died, and he was in love, yet again – this time with a married woman who only stood at a window in her marital home and waved. She'd only waved goodbye, I had only placed my arm around his shoulders and he immediately thought we were in love with him. Dear James, he was so sensitive. When I met her, we exchanged stories. Not unkindly, but with a shake of the head. As my mother often said about my father: 'He may be very clever, but he hasn't got much common sense!'

Chapter Seventeen

I was twenty one, I'd just finished my drama course at the Old Vic Theatre School, and I was one of four chosen to join the Old Vic Company. Margaret Chisholm, Norman Ayrton (who went on to run LAMDA; I'd been invited to his family home in north London. His family were Jewish and full of humour) and Ronnie Barlow, who took Donald's place.

We were rehearsing for *Twelfth Night* at the New Theatre in St Martin's Lane (afterwards renamed the Albery, then the Noël Coward. My last stage appearance was at this very same theatre, in *Calendar Girls*, but I'm hoping it won't be the last – 'latch on to the affirmative.') It was really exciting as the play was to star Sir Cedric Hardwicke, who had just come back from acting in Hollywood films, and it was to be directed by Alec Guinness. The actress who was to have played Viola wasn't really right for the part and I was told that Sir Alec had wanted me to take over because he had seen me as *Penthesilea*. The management felt that it would be too unkind to her to be replaced by someone completely new, so it didn't happen.

During one rehearsal I suddenly realised I was about to enter from the wrong side of the rehearsal room. I just knew I had to move before Alec saw me. I flew round the back of the slippery room, my beautiful brown silk dress billowing out like a flower; I was wearing high heels. As I slid to the ground in front of everyone, my only consolation was that it was a very graceful fall.

It was Alec Guinness's first time as a director and he came rushing up to me, very anxiously, 'Are you all right?' I rose to my feet swiftly and said, 'Yes, thank you.' I joined Maggie and the boys, and we followed our principals as they entered. As I said, I'm quite good at wriggling out of things!

It was during these rehearsals that I met my first husband, John Garley. He'd been an actor with the company for three years. When I met him, I saw him as a boyish-looking young man who was very amusing. He was playing Fabian in *Twelfth Night*, an ordinary, smallish part, but he made it funny and even his bare feet, size six, as befitted his height, seemed to twinkle as they moved quickly around the stage. I used to stand in the wings and watch his feet because they made me laugh. I still remember the way he spoke one line, as a little song, 'More matter for a May morning.'

He amused me. He was a very witty person. Doreen wrote in her diary: 'Went to see *Twelfth Night*, John Garley good. Revolutionary. Liked it.'

He was an incredible actor, very clever. Laurence Olivier

thought highly of his acting. In *King Lear* he gave him the stage by turning his head away from the audience, lowering his face and slightly sinking into himself when Johnny, playing the King of France, was proposing to Cordelia (played by Joyce Redman).

If I try to describe Johnny the words will sound wrong. I suppose his attractiveness lay in his personality.

He was in a play with Thora Hird at the Lyric Hammersmith once. It was written by Yvonne Mitchell and based on *Romeo and Juliet*. There was a chap in it who became very famous afterwards and he used to try to put Johnny down. He'd say: 'It's very hard to play a part that's boring without being boring isn't it?'

But Johnny was never boring. His personality informed his face, which was marred by a slightly receding chin and tip-tilted nose. Once when he was arriving back from a pre-London tour of *The Mortimer Touch*, I ran to the door to greet him, and when I saw him standing there I didn't recognise him. I saw his 'outside face', which was no longer familiar to me. Within ten minutes or so it was back to the face I knew and I no longer saw its faults.

We were great friends, Johnny and I, and that was all, really. He amused me and he thought I was beautiful, I suppose. That was probably all I had going for me at the time – I didn't have much wit, not many jokes, I was a very serious-minded young girl. Any relationship that might have been developing was more on his side, partly because I was still half involved with Donald, which was very difficult as he was away getting treatment for his mental illness and partly because there was also another man in the company whom

I was attracted to, Nigel Green. I felt a lot of sympathy for Nigel, his mother had been killed in a car accident, the loss of her affected him greatly and when he told me about it I felt a huge wave of sympathy which started my feelings of love towards him.

The people I was attracted to were all very different; all shapes, sizes and personalities.

Johnny was not impressed and he cut me off completely. He was strong-minded and fearless in all ways. He had never been to the Bond Street flat and I had no idea where he lived. I made no attempt to revive our friendship.

The rehearsals were for a four-week tour that opened at the Opera House, Manchester. It was there that my friend Margaret Chisholm and I were asked for our autographs for the first time. As my friend and I came out of the stage door after the first matinee, two small children, a boy and girl of about ten years old, asked for our autographs. We were only playing ladies-in-waiting.

'You won't want ours,' I said, 'We're not important.'

The boy, 'No, but you might be one day!'

We took them to tea with us at Duncan and Foster's Tea Rooms.

Waiting for us as we arrived at the stage door on the Saturday was the boy, who asked if he could see the stage. We took him in with us to look round it and up to our dressing room.

Then there was a knock on the door and Alec Guinness's voice said: 'May I come in?'

Just then, the call-boy announced 'the half hour call' and visitors were not allowed to be backstage after the 'half'!

We hid the boy under our dressing table and stood in front of him. Alec Guinness gave us our stage direction. So the boy only managed to catch a glimpse of Alec Guinness's shoes. When Alec had left we hurried him out through the pass door to the auditorium, so that he saw the play for the second time – this time for nothing. Many years later I discovered that the boy went on to become the creator and writer of *Coronation Street*, Tony Warren; I should have asked him for his autograph!

It was so hot in Manchester that year and caused the digs to smell of cat pee. My lovely pink linen dress became grey from the dusty air and it was an exhausting process to wash it by hand, rinsing it out, so heavy from the water, finding somewhere to hang it to dry and then ironing it. Jerseys were easier as they could be laid flat under the carpet between sheets of newspaper where the print stayed where it was meant to be (on the page, not on the clothes) and got pressed flat as we walked over it.

After the first night of *Twelfth Night*, the very next morning we started rehearsing for *Doctor Faustus*. I'd been cast as 'Sloth', one of the Deadly Sins, and 'The Vision, the Paramour of Alexander at the Court of Charles V'.

These were quite strenuous parts and full of movement. I had swapped roles with Josephine Stuart; instead of playing my own sin of Sloth – which would have been appropriate; I confess to having a lazy streak – I was to play Lechery. No, that's something I wasn't filled with!

Josephine was a sweet young girl, innocent. She wouldn't have been happy making advances to Sir Cedric Hardwicke as Doctor Faustus; she would have been so embarrassed. I wasn't. It was much more fun to crawl around and over Doctor Faustus than roll around on the floor getting dusty. We were both relieved.

My part of The Vision had no lines. So far, I had not uttered a single word in my first professional engagement. I was taught a danced mime by Sigurd Lieder, who had his own famous ballet company. He showed me that too much effort put into a twizzle would cause one to stagger and too little would be insufficient to complete a full turn. I could do it perfectly once but now my balance is not what it was. I was asked to do that great marathon of *Strictly Come Dancing* not so long ago and replied: 'Now, if you'd asked me ten years ago.'

I enjoyed the The Vision mime – I held my arms up, slightly bent at the elbows with my wrists almost together back to back and hands turned out and level, rather like Dame Shirley Bassey when she's performing. On occasion, when taken by the desire to impersonate her, this is what I do; only, I mime her powerful voice. Otherwise you'd think, what on earth does she think she's doing?

My costume fitting for The Vision was a strange experience. The tight, lined blue bodice was cut so that the two front pieces were joined by a centre seam. The costumier, taking a large pair of scissors, proceeded to cut two-thirds of the way down this seam, and as she did so my bare bosom emerged, slowly, like toothpaste being squeezed out of a tube. I was rather alarmed. But when she removed the top piece by cutting it to form a very wide U-shape, my bosom settled, thankfully, into its normal shape. Only, now, it was open to view.

For modesty's sake, not to mention appeasing the censor, this naked expanse was covered by a small strip of coffee-coloured net. As I was using coffee-coloured liquid makeup to tint my body, it became invisible. This rather defeated the object, and to all intents and purposes I was bare-breasted!

I have always been proud of the fact that in 1948, I was actually the first topless stage actress! I remember during the run of that play, a young actor was always coming up from behind (he was a very lively and attractive young man then) and I'd feel a pair of hands come around me and I'd say: 'Go away, Charlie!'

I knew exactly who it was – I know his wife, so I've got to be careful not to mention his real name.

We continued with the tour for the next three weeks, arriving exhausted in Leeds. Margaret (known as Maggie or Chissie, as her surname was Chisholm) and I, both equable girls, never showing temper, had become irritable and began to bicker. We were staying for the final week outside Leeds, at the family house of a student, Elizabeth, who'd also been at the Vic School, on the stage management course. We'd been sharing a room in digs and sleeping in the same bed. No one thought anything of it between friends then – it was the sensible thing to do, cheaper than two singles. I recall us bickering away, then her look of amazement. Her expression pulled me up and I realised how uncharacteristically we were behaving. We were tired, exhausted by the heavy rehearsals by day and the performances at night.

Now when I see unusual behaviour, I question whether it's because of fatigue and I make allowances. So although it was horrid at the time, it taught me not to react immediately but to hold back and try to see the reason for it.

I was a much nicer person then than I am now. It makes me sad to see a person change so much in their character because of setbacks in life. Most of us do it – myself included. In the case of Chissie and me, we were young. Once off that tiring tour, when she was back with her family in Enfield and I was back at the Bond Street flat, we became ourselves again, and from there on we were always good friends.

Back in London for our London opening night we'd been given a dressing room at the very top of the New Theatre. Pauline Jameson, who was playing Maria, and Penny Munday were on the same floor. Before the curtain rose, Alec Guinness gave Pauline a bouquet of flowers and us three girls – the walk-ons and understudies – were given a first-night gift of an inscribed book. Pauline, not knowing he'd given us a gift too, hesitated in front of Penny to thank Alec for her bouquet when he came round to wish us 'Good luck'. Afterwards, Pauline managed to catch him alone, and thanked him.

'They were dead when I gave them to you,' was his response. Much later, when he was very successful and confident, he was quite different but then he was easily rebuffed and had taken it as an insult that she had ignored his gift.

The season was supposed to run for a year at the Old Vic, including a visit to New York where *Twelfth Night* and *Dr Faustus* were to be taken. The disaster of Faustus made that impossible. Sir Cedric, very much admired in America, was the main attraction but Faustus had come off within a few performances, his main part had gone. Olivier had taken a company to Australia and had asked Johnny to go with him, and Ralph Richardson had gone to America. This meant that John Burrell was left to run the company, and I'm afraid that season was cut short, ending after six months.

We did have Dame Edith Evans being brilliant in *The Way of the World* and *The Cherry Orchard*, and Sir Cedric Hardwicke being wonderful in *Twelfth Night*, but on the other hand failing completely as *Doctor Faustus*. He didn't ever rehearse the last scene, which has those beautiful lines, 'See, where Christ's blood streams in the firmament! One drop would save my soul.'

He'd say: 'I'm working on this at home, John,' to the director.

It came to the first night and Sir Cedric, who attended him as his Wagner, said to Johnny, as they crossed together behind the back-cloth for Faustus's very emotional scene: 'I feel sick.'

His curtain call speech was: 'I would like to thank Sir Laurence for being in Australia and Sir Ralph for being in America.'

This got a very good laugh from the audience.

That production only lasted a few days.

I heard the news that The Arts Council were sending the play *Noah* out on a tour of Wales and when the interviews were being held I gatecrashed. My name wasn't on the list but even so I was sent in to see Alan Davies, the director. I thought I'd done quite well but went back to the Old Vic School to see if there was anyone who might help.

I met George who was in the canteen. He was always eating buns at the time; it was before he went on a diet a few years later.

'George, do you think I could play Naomi in *Noah*?'

'Yes'.

'Do you know Alan Davies?'

'Yes.'

'Would you give him a ring and tell him so?'

George promised he would do it straight away and so I was given the part of Naomi and would earn £10 a week! Twice my salary at the Old Vic Company.

Rosebud moved into the flat to be with Joycie while I was away for ten weeks and so began a joyous tour of Wales. We went to all the mining villages on our tour bus and sang or played silly games. The hoardings were a constant source of amusement. We'd see the Bisto Kids advertisement and shout, 'There they are!' or some girl, with a long neck, 'There she is!' It was a way of passing the time.

For the first two weeks we were based in Cardiff. Nigel Green was there in my first week on a pre-London tour. I met him for lunch one day and I was left feeling completely inadequate. A waiter had offered me something, I'd smiled and said:

'No, thank you, I don't like it.'

That was a faux pas, I was told it was unnecessary to say that I didn't like it. I gathered that the waiter should not have been accorded such familiarity. Walking back to my digs after lunch I noticed that I was walking pigeon-toed, my confidence obviously at a low ebb. I had the sense to decide that it was the last time that I would bother with him.

That evening on the bus taking us to one of our hospitable mining villages to perform in the village hall, Richard Pearson, who was playing Shem, announced to the cast: 'We've got all of June with us tonight!'

Very perspicacious of him to notice that I'd thrown off my shackles and was myself again.

Someone then remarked to Edward Jewesbury, who was playing Ham opposite my Naomi, 'I saw you in Smith's today.'

Edward replied: 'Yes there's a book I'm reading.'

I found this very amusing and saw him in a different light. It's a pity that I didn't notice this about myself at the time and it should have been obvious to me that I found men more compatible if their sense of humour coincided with mine. The attraction towards the ones for whom I felt sympathy was the wrong path for me to follow. It might have saved me from heartache.

I began to be interested in Edward, or Teddy as he was known. Standing in the wings one evening he put his hands on my hips, the following day we went together to the Cardiff Museum where we gazed at a replica of Rodin's *Le Baiser* translated (as I'm sure you know) as 'The Kiss'. I ran my hands over its beautiful curves. Teddy's problem was mine; he was a romantic.

He made a comment on that occasion that shocked me as I wasn't used to straight-forward remarks of that nature: 'I wonder how long it will be before we . . .' I said nothing.

We saw a film together. During it he leaned forward towards the screen, exclaiming: 'It's Julia!'

She was his previous and quite recent romance, I discovered. I should not have been so foolish but my sympathy was engaged immediately. It was misplaced as I found out that he was married with two little children. My sympathy should have been for her his wife.

Later, when I was enduring a deep unhappiness caused by rejection, I regretted my stupidity and felt very ashamed. When I realised this, I had what might be called a 'St Paul on the road to Damascus' revelation. It brought me face to face with my beliefs.

At the time though, I fell in love with him and we started an affair. We stayed at The Grapes Hotel in Llangollen and it seemed idyllic. We walked in the meadows, sailed paper boats on a stream and I was very happy.

It could only be an interlude of course, we were away from our usual surroundings and he from his responsibilities, but the tour ended and the affair went on. It ended in more heartache for me.

I was out of work now for the first time – but not the last – and I had no agent. I only had Doreen in London to discuss things with, as she was a junior instructress at the Vic School and she stayed often in the flat. Sheila Lader was living rent-free in the flat while Chrissie was on tour. Sheila was penniless and hadn't worked since we left school so wasn't eligible for what we called 'the dole'. I was, as I'd done six months' work. I took Sheila in and we lived on my dole money of £1.40 a week and my savings. I bought a cheap packet of ten cigarettes a day and we smoked five each. That fact will indicate how poverty stricken we were.

I wasn't very happy with my relationship with Teddy and Doreen worried about the same thing. She also worried about what would happen to her after her job at the school came to an end. It was during this period that Doreen and I were on a tube platform with Sheila when she walked purposefully forward towards the line, just as the train was coming out of the tunnel into the station. We grabbed one arm each and yanked her back. That made three of us in a poor frame of mind, but hers was by far the worst. She made another attempt at suicide a few years later and in that she succeeded. She was only in her twenties.

The one thing you need to have if you choose the acting profession is resilience. Acting was called 'the profession' then, not 'the business', it could be heart-breaking.

After a few weeks I gave Teddy up and remember walking along the Cromwell Road back to Rosebud's flat in tears. He contacted me a fortnight later: 'I'm in a play at The Boltons, will you come and see it?'

I did and saw not only Teddy but a new very young actress, Dorothy Tutin. I thought she was a complete actress. She was extremely good, everything was in place and I knew that she would be successful, which of course she was. I saw her play the French princess in *Henry V* at the Old Vic Theatre and she was enchanting. I saw her later in *St Joan* at the Lyric Hammersmith and I was to be in the series of *South Riding* with her in the Seventies.

Then Doreen and I went to see Teddy in *She Stoops to Conquer* at the Arts Theatre. He was better in this than he was in *Noah*. Seeing him unsettled me. The next day I had an audition with Hugh Hunt for something at the Adelphi Theatre.

I met Doreen at the Green Lizard tea room the next day

and told her the audition hadn't gone well; I was right because I never heard anymore.

Teddy and I would see each other for a while. I joined the Colchester Repertory Company for four plays very shortly afterward and he came once to see me for a day. We walked in the fields outside Colchester where we made love for the last time and were slightly disturbed by a solitary man walking past. Transport being sporadic, I got to the theatre by the skin of my teeth with fifteen minutes to make up and dress before curtain up.

We wrote to each other until a year later when I was to write telling him that I was marrying Johnny Garley.

There had been a spate of work for me after the Old Vic season collapsed as now I'd been offered a season in the Young Vic Company to tour England and the Continent.

I'd been living at home while I was at Colchester and played some marvellous parts there, Kay in *Time and the Conways* by J.B. Priestley, which I loved playing. I have always kept in mind the poem that her brother quotes to her, which is by William Blake:

> *Joy and woe are woven fine,*
> *A clothing for the soul divine.*

I left Colchester to go on the Young Vic tour, where I met up with Johnny again.

The Shakespeare for this season was to be *The Merchant of Venice* and I'd been offered Jessica. We toured all over the country. I remember a few towns because they had significance for me. For instance in one performance at the Library

Theatre in Manchester I played both Jessica and Portia. Jill Showell, a student just out of the Old Vic School second year, had come straight into the leading part of Portia in *The Merchant*. She was a girl with a sunny disposition but a bit too inexperienced to have been given that opportunity so soon. She had fair curly hair, looked right for the part of Portia. She wore a small, rather attractive-looking shaped cap, which covered her hair as Portia. It was rather a pity as you didn't see her hair, which, according to Bassanio, hangs down her back like a golden fleece. Of course, I wished they'd given Portia to me.

In this particular performance Jillie fainted at the end of the first act. I had just done the scene where Jessica donned her boy's costume as she rushed down from her upper window in her father Shylock's house to run away with Lorenzo, and that was a very quick change of costume.

The next time Jessica was seen, she was transformed into Portia entering with Bassanio and pleading with him not to choose the casket that will win her hand straight away but to wait so that she has more time with him in case he chooses the wrong one and she'll lose him forever.

There was a little murmur from the audience, which fortunately soon subsided. I enjoyed having an important leading part in a classical play and I did get a very good reaction to it, which was a solace for me. Joycie, my friend from the days of the Bond Street flat asked someone who'd seen the play, 'What was Jillie like?' and his answer was, 'She was off, I was lucky, I saw the understudy.' Twice in the provincial papers, the critics having given me a good notice as Jessica, wrote 'I would have liked to have seen her play Portia.' So would I, was my thought. So what, I played Portia once! Well twice, it had been a matinee with the evening performance to come.

It is when you're constantly understudying that you get dispirited, like a bird trapped in a cage. You'd understand if you were that poor actor who played Hamlet at the Old Vic in its infancy when it was run by Lilian Baylis. 'Well,' she said as he came off stage, 'you've had your chance and you've missed it!' Poor chap! I suppose it could have been his nerves. The story goes that she used to watch performances from the Stage Box, the smell from the sausages she was frying for her supper pervading the auditorium.

Talking of 'nerves', I was doing a short stint in *Coronation Street* in the Seventies as the boy organist's mother and as the cast was gathering to go into the studio, the actors were look-ing highly nervous. I said to Bill Roache, disbelievingly, 'They're not still nervous, are they?' They had been doing it for years, at least fifteen.

'Yes, it gets worse.'

I thought what a waste of time and decided never to be nervous again, but to do what you were always being urged to do just as you're about to go on stage, enjoy it! You think, 'Don't be stupid!' but it's right; that is, if you 'work for the work's sake!' I didn't understand it then, when it was in my school reports, I do now.

During this tour Johnny and I had become friends again. We went to the pictures, had tea together, and walked round the towns that were interesting or beautiful, like the univer-sity towns with their rivers and colleges. I don't think Johnny was interested in churches, we never discussed spiritual matters nor visited museums, but we talked. I listened as much as I talked but I think I listened more and learnt.

He was immersed in the theatre. He'd read everything he could about the old great actors and their theatre. He'd been acting, properly acting, giving solo readings of his father's adaptation of *Love on the Dole* and Dickens's *A Christmas Carol* since he was twelve. He filled the halls he performed in Kettering and around, he got front page headlines in the local papers. Much was expected of him.

If I were dispirited, Johnny had more cause to be. You would never have known from his outward behavior – full of high spirits – he enlivened every gathering. He saw the funny side of everything and did his impersonations, made his witty comments.

After he died, a young actor from the Stratford Company told me, 'We loved you both but were a bit frightened of Johnny.'

'Why?' I was astonished,

'He could demolish us with one line.'

'But never on purpose, he'd just see the laugh to be had!' I explained.

Johnny loved to be in the company of others like him, such as George Rose, and Alec Guinness until their friendship went awry. Alec was a very good impersonator but had been advised to stop doing it as it could mar his acting.

That was the man that I knew best. I knew something of his frustration but very little. I don't want to make him sound dreary, not self-pitying, because he was the opposite of that.

Picking up from where we'd left off, Johnny and I were soon on a short journey towards marriage – from October when the tour began until 24 February 1950, our wedding day. It started as a friendship, developing on the way, until one day our landlady knocked on the door and called, 'I've brought your breakfast up.'

I looked at Johnny lying beside me and mouthed, 'Get into the wardrobe.'

He leapt out of bed and shot inside it, I made sure the door was shut and then I ran back to bed, at which point there was a second knock.

This time her voice said, 'There's another breakfast on the landing.'

This sounds funnier if spoken with a Northern accent, which she had. When I told her later that we were getting married her attitude changed. This made it all above board. On another occasion in a different town when a knock came on the door, deciding that the wardrobe hiding-place would take too long to access, I hissed: 'Lie flat on your back!'

I hid him under the bedclothes. It worked!

Johnny got to know and like Doreen and would have confidential talks with her, asking how she thought he could get me to marry him. She told him, apparently, that I had said he was too soft. Upon which information he began to treat me in a high-handed, bossy way which didn't endear him to me at all. I found out the reason from him and promptly told him that wasn't the way. Once Johnny reverted to his normal behaviour he proposed to me. 'Maybe in two years' was my answer. The second time he asked me I said, 'Maybe in six months.'

When he asked me yet again I replied, 'Oh, let's get married now!'

Johnny knew that I was at the tail end of my involvement with Teddy, which still worried him. I'd seen Teddy that summer, gone to plays he was in and was keeping up a correspondence. I confided in Doreen, she helped me with a letter that I was sending to Teddy to tell him I was to marry Johnny. He insisted on seeing it, obviously not trusting me. I was unwilling to do that as I would have to give it an uncaring tone. But I gave in in order to pacify him, showed it to him, sealed and posted it in front of him. How obedient I was – I'd been taught to be.

So we bought a special licence, and as I was still on the electoral roll of my old church, St Mary-le-Tower in Ipswich, we were able to be married within a fortnight by the same Reverend Mr Babbington on whom Pauline and I had what might be termed our schoolgirl crush. The old saying 'Get married in haste, repent at leisure' did not apply in my case. I was very happy in my marriage, and unhappy when it ended.

Johnny bought me a beautiful pale-lemon gabardine coat with small black leather straps at the wrist and neck. I couldn't find a hat to match so I wore a small black one, with black shoes, bag and gloves – black, not an auspicious choice for a wedding. We only had rough proofs of the photographs as we couldn't afford the prints; they all turned sepia and faded away. Only my family were there and Johnny's mother.

Mrs Russell, Pauline's mother, came silently into the church and sat at the back. I had told her about the wedding, and although she knew it was only a small family affair, she told me when I saw her as we left, 'I couldn't know that you were getting married without being there.'

How unkind we were, leaving out friends and family. In the aftermath of the war, we'd become used to living our separate lives.

Our wedding breakfast would have been ham sandwiches and, most likely, sherry or tea at our house. I expect Mother had made a cake. Then Johnny and I had to make our return journey to Norwich to join up with the Young Vic Company for that evening's performance.

To my dismay, Mrs Garley seemed to assume that she would be coming with us. I looked at Mother, who said laughingly, 'Oh, you can't go with them on their honeymoon. You stay here with us and we'll see you on the train home tomorrow.' I was so grateful to Mother for picking up her cue so speedily.

Arriving back in Norwich, Doreen said I looked lovely and gave me the stockings she'd lent me the previous night for my wedding as mine had a ladder in one of them. We were given a clock as a wedding present. Was it an alarm clock – a subtle hint? After the performance we all went to a pub to celebrate and a wise old Norfolk man gave me his advice for life, 'Never worry, it impairs the efficiency.' That works very well unless others try to push you into worrying. My usual response is, 'It'll be all right, it'll be all right', and quite often it is.

Johnny and I had very few holidays, but we did have one that was a late honeymoon – in Cassis sur Mer, when it was still very undeveloped. We only went for a week as we couldn't afford more. We flew on a night flight from a London airport, probably Northolt to Paris, on a £10 return, and then took the train overnight to Marseilles, sitting up all the way; then we caught the local bus to the coast. Cassis was very quiet; there were two hotels, the Hôtel Liautaud was family-owned. We stayed there. Georgie Rose had written our letter to M. Liautaud for us in French as he'd stayed there the year before. I'd got a distinction in my French oral at School Cert (Oxford) level, but had no confidence in my French, so Georgie wrote it for us. The floors were marble and the local wine was 10p a bottle; the better wine was 20p.

There was a smell of pines, lavender, of Gauloise, Disque Bleu and Ambre Solaire. It wasn't possible then to buy that in England. We walked up into the hills, took trips out to sea on a pedalo, looking down through the transparent water to the seabed – so deep that I'd say, 'Let's go back Johnny!' The tops of Johnny's uncovered feet got sunburnt and I put vinegar and water on them.

It was the only holiday we ever had. We had to wait all day in Paris until the night flight back to Northolt. We wandered around – went into Notre Dame and sat in the square nearby. Johnny bought a large bottle of light beer, some bread and tomatoes, to last the day. He insisted that I visit Napoleon's tomb – I did, with our last few francs, but I'd rather have had a slice of ham to go with the tomatoes.

Sitting in a bar at the airport, Johnny met a man whom he knew, who offered us a drink. 'Coffee, please.' He looked startled – he'd meant alcohol.

Having nowhere to live after the tour will become a refrain – throughout our marriage, we lived in other actors' homes, except for the last time. After this tour we went to live in Soho Square with Peter Copley, whom we both knew from being with him in the Old Vic Company. He had a lovely flat. His wife, Pamela Brown, was away on tour and they had a spare room, all blue, brown, white and lovely. He had a daily woman who came in and she would bring us toast, Cooper's Oxford marmalade and real coffee for breakfast. We liked living there as we got on very well with Peter, because of our sense of humour. Actors in those days were full of humour and full of stories. There were actors like Georgie Relph, who was on the stairs at the New Theatre, talking to Joycie Redman (everyone's name was always pronounced with an 'ie' or 'y' on the end – Johnny, Joycie, Rosie; I was Junie. Although you didn't say Alecky for Sir Alec Guinness – we were respectful). Joycie gave a startled scream, 'Did you see that Georgie?'

'What?'

'A rat'.

'Oh, I thought it was my DTs again'.

If you don't know what that means, it's 'Delirium Tremens', hallucinations brought on by too much alcohol!

George Devine said to us one day when we were talking about Sir John, 'Why don't you call him John amongst your-selves?'

'Because we don't call him that to his face.'

Peggy Ashcroft, we would never call her anything but 'Miss Ashcroft'. She loved the young members of the company and we always used to go out with her. Once in Liverpool she took us all off to try to find opium – she was asking all the waiters where we could get some opium! She never found any.

I forgot myself on a plane one day; we were touring in Germany, and I said to her without thinking, 'Come on, Peggy.' And then I said, 'Oh, I'm so sorry!'

And she said, 'Why?'

'I called you Peggy.'

'Of course you must call me Peggy,' she replied.

So then I did. After she became a Dame I was still able to call her Peggy.

On our wedding anniversary of 24 February Johnny always gave me lilies-of-the-valley, which were out of season. When we were on tour together we'd eat out once a week, always, when we got paid, but not when we were at home. I would buy myself a very special packet of cigarettes on pay day, such as Passing Clouds or Player's Gold Leaf, which held twenty-four in the packet, or Player's No. 1 that had '20 Pieces' printed on it. We'd find the best restaurant in the town and go there after the Friday performance. It would be English food, like lamb chops, steak or calves' liver, not pasta. I was very good at making steak and kidney pie and casseroles. We weren't regular drinkers; I don't remember ever having a bottle of alcohol in the flat. We just used to drink occasionally after the performance with the other actors in the theatre bar or a pub.

When I was married living in London I used to do the housework. Johnny would help me make the bed, though. In those days you didn't have men doing housework, but he would help me do the bed because it was such a chore. It wasn't a duvet like we all have now – it was sheets and blankets. We didn't own any bed linen, it was already in the flats vacated by their owners, actors away on tour.

We would often stand in the bedroom when in our digs with our arms round each other, mine inside his jacket, and stand face to face and talk for half an hour before we went to bed.

He was a very warm and generous person but he had two failings. One, he had a temper. It was a rather blustering sort of a temper and it was soon over. Two, he couldn't accept an apology. I mean, if you said to him, 'Oh, I'm terribly sorry!' he would say, 'Yes well . . . You shouldn't have . . .' He would continue it. So the only way to get on an even keel again was for me to twist it round, make it so that *he* was in the wrong and he would apologise to me. Then I would say, 'Oh, that's all right.' And it would all be over!

If we had an argument or row, I would go off and sleep on the sofa, he would always come after me. I remember one night he didn't and I was getting so cold on the sofa that I got up and went back to the bedroom – and he'd fallen asleep. I was so cross.

There was a little fleapit of a cinema in Notting Hill Gate and Johnny adored Charles Laughton's acting, so we would go to see *Mutiny on the Bounty* and *The Hunchback of Notre Dame*. I would always acquiesce. I didn't say, 'Oh, I want to see this film or that film.' I would always do what he wanted. I was a very amenable person in those days. It used to cost a couple of bob to go to the pictures. We didn't have a television set; I think we had a radio. Oh – we had a car . . . and our car was our freedom. Johnny was a very companionable man – if we were driving somewhere I could have a lot of different men in the car with me: I had Winston Churchill, Ralph Richardson, Olivier . . . Alec Guinness and Georges

Guétary, the French singer/actor – 'Sing like Georges Guétary,' I'd say.

London had thick smogs. One winter, we were living in the basement of the Reteys' house in Holland Street, and the fog was the worst I'd seen. You really couldn't see your hand in front of your face. We got into the car and I drove very slowly up to the top of Highgate Hill, the fog cleared and there was brilliant sunshine. We looked back and the whole of London was covered in a yellow cloud, just like a bowl of pea soup.

Sometimes we'd go to Johnny's parents' house or we'd go to my parents'. They loved him in Ipswich. It was always fun and laughter when he was there; my mother loved him, my sisters loved him and so did my father.

I drove, he didn't, but he always praised me. He used to say, 'Isn't she beautiful? Isn't she marvellous? She's so clever,' and 'She's such a wonderful driver'. I was so used to being praised that there was this terrible sense of loss and loneliness when the love was taken away.

Chapter Eighteen

I have had a very difficult jigsaw puzzle in front of me made up mostly of blue sky and dark green foliage. I can't fit the pieces together. To misquote Eric Morecambe, they're right pieces – but not necessarily in the right order!

It's the two Young Vic Company's overseas tours that have me flummoxed. My dear friend Doreen kept a diary all her life and in 2008 I asked her for her help when I restarted to re-write this book – if I dare call it that. (The first few chapters having been written in 2001.)

So, in 2008, Doreen gave me the snippets that concerned both her and me of our years at the Old Vic School and the first Young Vic tour, unfortunately she wasn't in the second tour and I was – and therein lies my difficulty.

Events in her year don't tie up with my being married

or single. If you'd kindly not try to unravel this, neither will I.

So here goes.

When we were in Holland with the Young Vic Company we stayed in the house of a Dutch millionaire and his wife, who were giving private hospitality to members of the cast. We were the lucky ones. Herr and Frau van Gelder had a beautiful house, and the terrace went down to the well-tended lawn. The first morning Johnny and I went down to have breakfast and on the sideboard were strawberries and cream and we put them in small silver bowls.

Herr van Gelder came in and said, 'Oh dey are de finger bowls'.

We obviously weren't used to the high life. The butler definitely knew we weren't because he'd unpacked our cases!

I walked around the garden with Herr van Gelder, possibly after the incident of the finger bowls that morning and remarked, 'So, you haven't got much land . . . ?' 'Only four acres but I share a shoot of forty acres with a friend.' I don't think I added more to the conversation, not being at my brightest that day. I certainly didn't mention that my father had once owned a shoot of four acres!

Frau van Gelder told me that she always stayed at Claridge's when in London as it was only one or two pounds a day more. I didn't tell her that once we'd stayed at the Cumberland for only seventy-five pence. I was learning my lesson – think before you speak or keep quiet. She was a very charming woman.

Frau Van Gelder was a true aristocrat, although her

husband was from the business world. He owned a newspaper in Amsterdam and half the Amstel Hotel (he was pretty wealthy). In fact when he dropped us off in Amsterdam one day so that we could do some shopping he asked, 'Would you like some money?' and we said, 'Oh no thank you.'

In fact we'd have loved some but we would never have admitted it.

One evening Frau van Gelder said, 'Would you mind having your meal without us tonight?' They had dined earlier than their usual hour because of our having to go off to the theatre to do the play, *A Midsummer Night's Dream* in that wonderful open-air theatre in Bloemendaal.

On this occasion she told us that they had guests that night, so we ate on our own and I sat in Frau van Gelder's place with her bell to summon the butler.

I duly rang the bell and in came the butler already dressed up in preparation for waiting on the Van Gelders and their guests later. He wore a white frilly shirt and his tails.

He came in the door – I have to illustrate this – I was sitting in Frau's chair and Johnny was sitting there in his usual place at this big round table and the butler did this low bow, his hand giving three twirls until it almost reached the floor. We laughed and continued to play the whole dinner as a comedy. We, as master and mistress of the house and he, our servant who gave us this deep bow each and every time he entered with the next course. I reciprocated with a gracious inclination of the head. It was a mimed performance, we didn't speak each other's language but we laughed a lot. It was the jolliest dinner we had there.

*

In Sweden our hosts were rather cold – a grim theatre director and his wife but the two sons were friendly. Nils Larson was an actor and his brother a painter.

He took us to an exhibition of paintings of natural landscapes by an American, each one sketched over by a tracery of spider's webs – I was not impressed by them, wondering what they were supposed to represent. I can still see the tracery of cobwebs all over them but not the pictures themselves. Now I wonder if they presaged the World Wide Web – a web covering the whole of our world of which I am wary. A very useful tool if you are seeking information but even that can be anybody's interpretation.

After one performance at Bloemendaal I was running swiftly down the hill to reach the stage with my Theseus, Mervyn (Butch) Blake, spear aloft, when a muscle gave way in the back of my left thigh. It was very hard to keep my leg straight but I managed somehow to keep on performing this strong Amazon. Dr Greasepaint must have arrived. Edith Evans's panacea for all ills.

Dear 'Frau' paid a physiotherapist to come to their mansion to put my leg to rights. I don't remember having any more trouble with it at that performance nor any afterwards, the physio must have been very skilled and very expensive I should imagine, knowing how wealthy the van Gelders were.

We visited them when we were in Amsterdam on the overseas Stratford Memorial Theatre tour, taking them two large vacuum-sealed tins of Lyons ground coffee. It was the only thing that was impossible to get in their country, filled as it was with an abundance of food. Our gift was received with delight, I had redeemed myself.

Moving on, we travelled by train to Denmark and stayed with a lovely young couple in their very beautiful modern house. She was a fashion artist and I still have a sketch that she drew of me hanging on my wall. I heard later that I'd passed on a very bad cold to their baby which developed into pneumonia and she nearly died.

Apart from the constant round of parties and the reception at the British Embassy, we visited the famous Tivoli Gardens.

On to Stockholm, the beautiful city-on-the-water where Doreen and I wandered around a clothes store, talking to each other in mock Swedish which were gibberish spoken with a very high-class accent. It could have been taken for their Swedish except that it couldn't be understood. It was assumed that it was Finnish.

I don't recall Johnny getting up to any mischief, he must have been wanting to get home to familiar food and surroundings. He told me that when in New York he sat all day in a cold bath because he couldn't stand the heat. A friend of his joked that in the winter he went to bed in his teddy bear coat.

In those days actors wore more flamboyant dress than the general public. I had to tie his bow ties for him because he never got them to sit right and he always wore a waistcoat, either his checked one or the yellow velveteen one that I bought him.

Nowadays, he would have appeared as normally dressed as everybody else, as the ordinary public often look more eccentric than actors.

We were frugal with our money, always 'saving for a rainy

day', a euphemism for being out of work. We never used the term 'resting' as it didn't describe accurately our state of worrying about where the next job was coming from and how long our savings would last out.

Oslo was our last port of call, in all its vivid green, yellow and red autumnal colours, where we boarded the boat back to England. The Captain told us that if the door of the saloon slid shut it would be the sign of heavy seas, rough weather. It did exactly that. I went up to sit on the deck and watched the mountainous waves rise to the height of skyscrapers and then sink back down to sea level. It was fascinating.

At breakfast the next morning there was only myself and Edgar Wreford, who'd been a fellow student at the Vic school. We were amazed at the abundant food spread out on a long buffet table, and took part heartily.

Unfortunately Johnny was below in our cabin, not responding well to the weather, with the rest of the company. He was not a good sailor and I was to be ministering to a land-lubber lying down below.

That Christmas we had to spend with Mrs Steele in Hereford as it was impossible to get home. They were wonderful digs, which we shared with Lauchie McLean (an actor in the company) and Butch, my Theseus. Mrs Steele, who was stone deaf, provided us with a full breakfast no matter how late we came down for it followed by lunch at 1 p.m. tea at 5 p.m. and supper when we got back, however late. It was lucky that Johnny was on dry land.

She excelled herself on Christmas day, providing us with everything we would have had at home. It was just as well she couldn't hear or we might have kept the poor worn-out soul awake with our talking till two o'clock in the morning. Actors call this night-aliveness 'winding down'. Which is why you'll see actors go straight to the pub after curtain-down to avoid inflicting it on their families or just to have a jolly good time. 'See you in the pub' is heard issuing from the dressing rooms, never 'goodnight'.

Hereford was a hive of gossip that year. It had been found out that the all-male club called The Fifty Fifty was exactly that. The husbands had a lot of explaining to do to their wives. It was the topic of the town.

In Manchester we stayed with the Misses Finn, elderly Irish sisters who went to Mass in the Catholic church opposite. They had a shillelagh in the hall-stand.

These digs were four pounds a week, a cut above the cheaper ones of three pounds, and we were given a sitting room as well as a bedroom.

One night our bedroom door was flung open and the light switched on. One of the Misses Finn stood there, looking anxious, 'Is she having a nightmare?' I kept my eyes tight shut pretending to be peacefully asleep and left Johnny to deal with it. 'Yes,' he said, 'but she's all right now.' Off she went reassured and we hid our laughter under the bed-clothes.

We had taken *The Merchant of Venice* to the Old Vic Theatre in Waterloo Road for a season, as the Old Vic Company were performing in Brighton. There was a scare as a few cases of smallpox had been diagnosed there and Johnny was worried that some of the staff might return to London bringing the disease with them. He had never been vaccinated against it as I had when I was a baby. He was a bit of a hypochondriac.

Off I went with him to St George's Hospital then at its original site at Hyde Park Corner – now occupied by a hotel, The Lanesborough. It was very old, quite a dirty looking place but with two very cheerful informal young doctors who attended to us.

One dropped his needle on the floor – picked it up, wiped it off and used it to vaccinate Johnny. Only a tiny blister came up on my left arm, my old vaccination was still protecting me after twenty-two years, but Johnny's was a different matter, a large, extremely painful blister appeared on his.

I don't think it was because of the needle being dropped on the floor and hastily retrieved but because it was his first vaccination and was giving him a dose of cowpox but it had been a jolly little social occasion and Johnny bore the pain with stoicism. Nobody caught smallpox.

Lauchie McLean was staying where we were in Reading. This was, we thought, a converted monastery where we ate at a large round heavy oak table in a room with stained glass windows. We believed it had been the monk's chapel.

One night after a show as we sat having supper swapping ghost stories, I told them of my experience at the Borely Rectory in Suffolk when suddenly there was a sharp loud knock under the table as if it has been made with a heavy gold ring.

The reaction was spontaneous; everyone leapt out of their chairs and backed away. There was no laggard, no one had the time to retrieve their arm from under the table. 'We'll hold a seance,' Lauchie informed us. He was clairvoyant. Down we sat, Lauchie closed his eyes and began to do heavy breathing, then his eyes shot open looking most weird as if he wasn't there and fixed their sightless gaze on Johnny.

Johnny was suffering from the effects of the vaccination. We were both alarmed, thinking he'd be focusing straight on us. I concentrated on the table saying there's my packet of Goldflake and my matches, apparently Johnny was doing the same thing so we must have put up a barrier and ruined his seance because it came to an end. There were eight of us and one of the others said that Tom, our Australian stage manager, had also gone into a trance, so thank goodness we concentrated on normality, otherwise I would have been even more alarmed.

After two years of continuous work Johnny and I were faced now with trying to find a new job. Johnny had been offered to take his solo performance of *A Christmas Carol* to the cities of The Hague and Amsterdam by Jan de Blick, the Dutch impresario who was responsible for taking the Young Vic Company to Holland.

We had first class tickets on the boat and would be given private hospitality when we arrived. I had bought a white swing-coat for the coming winter, it was checked with lines of red and black. Deciding that it wasn't in the latest style I had made button holes down the front and attached black buttons, a small black rabbit fur collar to stand up from the neckline and fur cuffs. Unfortunately, it didn't sit right at the front as the edges weren't straight but cut on a curve which caused my button-up fastening to buckle between each button-hole.

So, carrying our heavy leather travelling bags (I didn't carry mine of course, Johnny having been brought up to have good manners carried both), we embarked for Den Haag each with our first class ticket. Settled comfortably in the first class saloon happily having a drink, we were approached by some official-looking man who enquired if we were in the right part of the boat. We showed our first class tickets and he retreated looking nonplussed. My black rabbit fur trimmings and button-holes failing the test. We would have been in steerage like the Irish in The Titanic if it had not been for Jan de Blick.

Arriving at The Hague we were taken to our private hospitatility where we found ourselves billeted on a very nice quiet man and his wife. During our stay with them we were told that he had been a member of the Dutch underground and had made many journeys into Belgium and France carrying information, posing as a deaf-mute. A courageous man.

Johnny was a great success. I assisted with the lights and making his performance run smoothly. He didn't need a prompter. He'd performed it before large audiences since he was twelve years old. He was an exceptional actor. One critic of the Dutch press had written that every young actor in Holland should go and see this young actor! They would have learnt a lot about the craft of acting from him as I did. Finally, he had the stage to himself – a joy to him after playing Young Gobbo instead of Shylock, a young lover instead of Truffaldino, and Puck instead of Oberon in the Young Vic tour.

George Devine realised his talent when he saw his understudy performance of Shylock, he said, 'I see what you mean, Johnny.'

We returned with our first class tickets to Harwich and went to live in our next rented flat – that of Mark Dignam. He and Peter Copley were both departing on a tour of Europe and Pam Brown was back in Soho Square so it was South Hampstead for us. There were many of these tours, to Paris, South Africa, Canada, Australia, places where it had been impossible to go during the war.

Somehow, through whom I don't know, I was asked to audition for Olivier to understudy Charmian to Vivien Leigh's Cleopatra on their next tour of Australia and New Zealand. Olivier went so far as to say, 'Is she too tall for Vivien?' but Pat Leigh, who was Olivier's personal dresser, told us that it was Lovat Fraser, his business manager, whom Johnny had also got on the wrong side of, who had put Olivier off employing me saying, 'She'll only get homesick for Johnny' and put the tin lid on that.

Olivier was known as the master of false noses and Johnny had said to me beforehand, 'Tell him to use plasticine!' After I'd done this audition, Olivier said to me, 'How's Johnny?'

I said, 'Oh, he's fine, but he said to tell you, "You want to use plasticine not nose putty for noses".'

He replied, 'Isn't that very difficult?'

'Oh no, it's really very easy.'

And he threw back his head and laughed, because here was I telling this man, a master of false noses from Richard III onwards, how to make one! Me, a young woman, who wanted to play beautiful parts, who'd never attempted a false nose – there was never a thought of a character actress in my mind! He was a lovely man.

Johnny had told me that he'd gone to see Olivier, after the Old Vic season ended early and put us both out of work in 1948, to see if he had a job for him. Olivier had always been so interested in him and his work but he was met with a very frosty reception. Olivier took him to task for not going with him and his company on the Australian tour, finishing his diatribe with, 'I didn't want a company of geniuses but good solid actors', to which Johnny replied, 'Then you must have been very happy', at which Olivier went red with rage. Johnny was awfully good at shooting himself in the foot. You couldn't help but laugh though!

Staying in South Hampstead I was introduced to Oscar Lewenstein through Renée Goddard, a very good actress whom I met during an audition. It couldn't have been of much importance or I'd remember what it was for. She was meeting Oscar after work and took me with her. I found him an interesting man and introduced him to Johnny. He and Eileen, his partner at the time, lived five minutes away from Mark's flat and we'd go and visit them often.

Oscar was a Communist but enjoyed reading the Old Testament in his large Bible, the history of the Jewish people, of course. He was a small bird-like man with interest in his eyes and we got on extremely well.

Oscar gave up his membership of the Communist Party later. It could have been his disgust at the behaviour of the Russians at the time of the Hungarian uprising or the fact that he'd become an impresario, perhaps both.

He married Eileen extremely reluctantly, in a suit, looking very grumpy, neither in a synagogue nor a church, but in a register office. Nevertheless it led to a long and contented marriage resulting in two little red-haired boys. Our differences in attitudes to politics and spiritual matters did not concern us, which is how it should be – tolerance is all.

I'd no idea at first that he was the manager of the Embassy Theatre in Swiss Cottage (now the Central School, whose training follows that of the Old Vic School. It was taken there by one of the fourth-year students, George Hall, who became their director). Not knowing this, I talked freely to Oscar, treating him as a person of no great importance to my future career. I only found out who he was when he offered me the part of the Jewish girl in *The Emmanuel Story* with the same theme as *Romeo and Juliet*. She was Jewish and the man she loved was a goy, a gentile. Lily Kahn and Martin Miller, two well-known Jewish actors, played the parents. I can hear him saying to her as they look up at the sky, 'Look, how many stars.'

She replied, 'There are more stars in Jerusalem', with magic in her voice.

How little of that is around today, now we act in such a matter-of-fact way.

I was given a lovely notice by Kenneth Tynan writing in the *Spectator*. He had not yet become well known as the theatre critic of the *Evening Standard*. If he had been that might have been a wonderful help to my career; Nigel Hawthorne was to write in his autobiography that he, a member of the stage management at the Embassy Theatre at the time, thought that I was the most beautiful young actress that he had seen on the stage. Lack-a-day; all 'if onlys'.

Johnny was about to start rehearsals for *The Same Sky*, a play by Yvonne Mitchell at the Lyric Hammersmith based on the same *Romeo and Juliet* theme. He played the Jewish boy in love with a Jewish girl who was in love with a gentile. Johnny's character was a tobacconist and he avoided having to smoke, as he was a non-smoker, by getting out a packet of cigarettes, turning it round in his hands several times and replacing it in his pocket. No one noticed that he didn't smoke once. There's always a way round everything. He was excellent as usual.

I'd already worked on a film at Pinewood Studios; it was *All About Eve,* which starred Jane Hilton, who was a promising up-and-coming actress from the J. Arthur Rank charm school. It was meant to be her big chance but the film was poor and therefore didn't advance her in the way she'd hoped. It happens to us all, as a lot of actors know to their cost. I said to Michael Cashman, my friend, 'The cream doesn't always rise to the top Michael.'

To which he replied, 'No, but the shit does!'

That's not quite true, but I laughed.

I started on my round of acting in the little theatres playing good parts to no avail.

Johnny had just finished playing in the West End in *The Mortimer Touch* directed by George Devine. Pam Brown was in the cast and meeting her after the performance she said, 'Poor Marie, a very slow actress. The trouble with her is she thinks when she's acting. Well you've done all your thinking in rehearsal haven't you.' Another good piece of advice for me to add to that of Dame Edith, 'It's like music, you have to give each other the right note, I can't do it without you and you can't do it without me, it's like music you see, dear'.

Johnny went immediately into a tour of *Seagulls over Sorento,* with a very good amusing set of actors and we made four good friends. Gerald Harper became his great mate, Barry Keegan the same; both young, single men and Barry Letts, who was known as Bart, another. Bart had a lovely wife, Chummy, who seemed to have no other forename but that. As I went with Johnny on the tour and Chummy, was often with Bart, she and I became companions and the four of us remained friends.

Gerald and Barry both had a sense of humour that appealed to Johnny and it was there that 'The Premier' and Anthony Eden came into existence, with Johnny and Gerry, which he transferred to himself and my father later on. I was fond of them all. Bart was often with us in the digs and he and I would discuss books and general subjects, not just acting, staying up talking often after Johnny had gone to bed.

There was yet another memorable landlady of a large pub in Derby where Johnny and I stayed together with Bart, Chummy and Gerry. This landlady had a gambling habit; she'd bet every day. You'd hear her on the phone in her high, swooping voice, 'I'll have five pounds on the nose.' Gerry would always ask her how her horse had fared just to hear her say, 'It got b-e-e-e-at,' in a long, drawn-out tone of surprise. That was Gerry's favourite amusement!

Bart also went through a phase where he played the horses. He had a kitty of fifty pounds which he used for his gambling. Chummy had put a cap on it for safety's sake. Bart had a system. The problem was he needed to be at the races for it to have any chance of succeeding. You backed the second favourite. The second favourite normally appeared on the betting boards just before the race so you can see his problem. He gave it up after a little while.

I could understand Chummy's wariness as when Bart was on the month's overseas part of the tour, he had asked for his salary to be paid to Chummy and it didn't arrive in the bank so she, being penniless, had only enough to feed her cats and drink water herself. It had two advantages, she lost weight and the dark circles under her eyes disappeared completely.

There was a slight fracas between Gerry and Chummy one lunchtime when he put his finger in the cream decorated trifle to taste whether it was real cream. Chummy was upset; she didn't think it was hygienic. That was the only disagreement I remember from any of the tours. We all seemed to get on very well.

It was during the tour of *Seagulls* that I went back home to Ipswich, as we had no home in London and my cousin John Templey taught me to drive. He was very good at this and much later had a driving school of his own which he told me shot his nerves to pieces.

He was fine with me and made sure I always watched the other drivers on the road. 'It's not you I worry about June but watch the other fellows in case they make a mistake', and I have ever since.

On a night drive in a country lane a car approached with very bright lights.

'Watch the road for me, John, I can't see.'

'Right-ho,' he said. It passed us.

'Neither could I,' admitted John, laughing.

After this tour of Germany mother had developed phlebitis. She had a habit of leaving her right leg dangling over her side of the bed when the covers became too hot for her. Father and she were Jack Spratt and his wife in this respect – and many others. In fact this phlebitis – which we now call deep-vein thrombosis' – entailed bed-rest, so I stayed to run the house and look after her. Rosebud was on a tour of *Lilac Time* and Lois was working at the bank. During this time I saw a lot of Roy Hullis, a friend of both Rosebud and Lois, in his last years at veterinary college.

Roy helped me redecorate Mother's kitchen – well, breakfast room. It had no kitchen appliances, only the 'Ideal' boiler. We scraped the gloss paint off the walls and woodwork with blocks of pumice and repainted the walls, originally half yellow and half brown, in Wedgwood blue with white woodwork – my decor obviously influenced by Peter Copley!

It was a very laborious job and left me with fibrositis in my right shoulder. Johnny threw cold water over my back later thinking I'd enjoy it. I didn't as it brought on another spasm. I had to sit with my back to a gas fire for days to help it to heal. We gave the dark-stained wooden wall clock, an American Quaker design, a coat of scarlet to give a bit of contrast, ruining the value of the clock in the process. Father didn't notice and he'd bought it.

I suddenly received a telephone call from the Piccolo Theatre Company in Manchester from Caspar Wrede, a Finn, who'd been on the directors course of the Old Vic School. He was a Count in Finland but only a few people knew that, as he didn't use his title in England. I did know because his wife, Dilys Hamlet, had been a student at the school and told me that on a visit to Finland the little children had curtsied to them as they passed. The gist of the phone call was that the actress playing the young girl's part in *The Women Have Their Way* had dropped out of rehearsals and would I replace her immediately.

It was on a sunny Shrove Tuesday in February that I set out from Ipswich to drive to Manchester, a long, long way in the days of no motorways. I'd passed my driving test six months before and had only driven around the town and the local countryside.

Approaching Kettering I was worried that there was something amiss with the car engine as there was an odd knocking sound so I stopped at a garage there to have it checked over. The garage found nothing wrong, so I set off again. By this time it was beginning to get dark and even worse, it started to snow. I'd never driven in the snow and unbeknownst to me my tyres were bald. My windscreen wiper was attached to the roof and cleared a nine-inch semi-circle downward just in front of my eyes. Apart from that the whole windscreen was covered with snow. On a main road all the cars and lorries flashed their headlights as I approached them, the headlights were set high on my car. 'I *am* dipped, I *am* dipped' I kept saying with despair. Turning left on the way to Rugeley I came to a fork in the road, which I couldn't see and stopped at the hedge dividing two roads.

A new 1953 model car drew up just ahead of me on the right-hand road. Someone got out and came towards me, 'Oh dear, he's going to bawl me out,' I thought, for being a woman driver and a poor one at that.

A very good-looking man stopped at my window. 'Is there anything wrong?'

'I can't see!'

'Where are you going?'

'Manchester, well, Chorlton-cum-Hardy.'

'I'm going there, follow me.'

I was so thankful. Off he drove with me following. I tried to keep up but he was doing fifty mph. My bald tyres didn't hold the road and on a slight bend I went into a four-wheel skid to the right, I tried to correct it, got into a four-wheel skid to the left then to the right again and then to the left. I zigzagged down the road and gave up. I had no seat belt, I just took my feet off the pedals, my hands off the wheel and sat calmly, waiting for the crash. I was completely calm thinking, 'Let it crash, at least I'll stop' and it did. It hit the bank on the left head-on – how it did that I've no idea – swung round facing across the road to the opposite bank, fell over on to its right side upon which I switched off the engine, left the lights on and taking the key with me, opened my passenger door and clambered out. I was unharmed except for slight bruises on my right side where I fell against the driver's door.

A red telephone box was slightly to the left of me on the bank into which the car had ploughed moments earlier, with a telegraph pole beside it. On the right was a five-barred gate leading into a field.

I was in the telephone box about to call 999 when the road behind me filled with lorries and bringing up the rear was my 'knight in shining armour' who, noticing I'd disappeared from behind him, had done a U-turn to see what had happened to me.

I didn't make my phone call; I got into his car whereupon he drove us to a pub and bought me a brandy. I don't remember giving my details to anyone but I obviously did because the lorry drivers had righted my car and pushed it into the field through the handy five-barred gate. My rescuer told me he was a Michelin tyre salesman and on the way to Manchester offered to put his car into a four-wheel skid to illustrate how to correct it. I politely declined this offer – I'd had enough of skids that night. I've been fearful of driving in the snow at night ever since.

I have done it accidentally. I once inadvertently led – with my five children in the car – a stream of cars on to a motorway slip road. I can't remember how we got out of that. I must have done a U-turn and led them all back.

This sounds as if I were a bad driver. I wasn't, I was a very good one, then.

Having just taken over the driving from my second husband once, with the same five children in the car, a tyre suddenly sprang a leak. Bob woke up.

'We've got a flat.'

'I know,' I said, manhandling the car, 'what do you think I'm doing on the hard shoulder?'

My small son wrote in a school essay detailing this occurrence, 'It was a good job mummy was driving.' He must have heard me say it to Bob.

Back on the road to Chorlton-cum-Hardy I had a lovely warm journey with music playing and a pleasant companion. I thanked him as he dropped me off at my digs and waved him goodbye.

The next morning Marriott Longman arrived to visit and take me with her to the Piccolo Theatre. I thanked her for coming and her offhand reply was, 'Oh, I wouldn't have come, they made me'. This sweet, quiet young woman who'd worked as an assistant instructress at the Old Vic School, had been married to Pierre Lefèvre, also from the school staff and one of the leaders of the Young Vic Company that I'd been in, had changed into this unsympathetic person. I'd lent her my bosom support that I used for Foible when she went on as understudy for Mistress Millamant and I left myself without my pouter-pigeon bosom, it had dropped without its support and I felt defenceless without it! I mean, one good turn deserves another. I'd made a sacrifice for her. She could have pretended to be concerned. Then I remembered that she and Pierre were divorced and she had loved him and lost her trust in him so I just laughed and said, 'Thanks all the same.'

I did love those weeks at the Piccolo. It was a church hall that the company stage management and actors alike were turning into a colourful theatre. They'd draped long swathes of striped black and white cotton material from the top of the high-pitched roof to droop in curves to the walls which acted as baffles for the sound and lowered the roof-space for intimacy. They were painting the upright chairs gold.

We helped with the props. I sat up late one night making an actor's padding. It was like being back at the Vic School, a group theatre. Richard Negri, the designer, painted big red dots on my white frilled Spanish skirt in the wings ten minutes before the curtain went up on the first night. I loved my part of Juanita La Rosa and the play. My Michelin-tyre salesman had turned up to see how I was the day after I'd waved him goodbye. His car was in the car park after rehearsal. It was dark so I went and sat with him in the warmth of the car. Then he put his arms around me and started to kiss me, 'No, don't, I can't, I'm married.'

He stopped and laughed.

'You're like a frightened little bird.'

I remember only that remark and the one about showing how to correct a skid. He was a nice man and very attractive.

By the time Johnny came back from his second tour in Ireland of *Seagulls Over Sorrento*, my play was finishing and we collected our mended car. It looked the same, the bodywork untouched. It had landed on several inches of snow and only the right-hand kingpin had been broken.

When I drove it, the steering didn't feel right so we took it to an AA checkpoint. The kingpin hadn't been replaced when we'd had the car repaired. It could have turned over yet again.

Seagulls Over Sorrento resumed its tour of England and Scotland.

It was when I was touring with Johnny again after this long gap, due to his foreign tours and my mother's illness, that I noticed Gerry and Johnny's closeness. It was friendship, nothing more, as if they were very fond brothers but I felt as if I were an intruder. Johnny was cross with me as I was walking along a beach in front of them, quite a long way in front, and he wanted to know why I'd walked off. I hadn't walked off; I'd been enjoying walking by the sea on my own. That was the only time he ever misunderstood me. I think it was then that I said, 'I don't think you need me here, I might as well go.' I thought I could go back to London and look for work. I wasn't jealous. I liked Gerry; we got on well.

Johnny and I had bought a used car, a Morris Series E, after I'd passed my driving test in Ipswich. I knew quite a lot about the inner workings of old cars through Uncle Billy. I'd been with him in his garage acting as his 'mate' often enough!

Gerry was helping me when we were in Bath, trying to fit a new accelerator spring to this car, from the accelerator pedal to the carburettor. The engine was revving up very loudly. A man passed by and I called out 'do you know anything about cars?' He turned out to be a motor mechanic and he slowed it down for me.

On occasion we'd go with Gerry to the golf course and after a quick look round he'd teach me how to do a golf swing.

I met with him and his girlfriend a few weeks after Johnny died and we drove down The Mall in his open Morris Minor following an official-looking car with its bull horn blaring out, 'Make way for the Spanish Ambassador!' We followed shouting, 'Make way for us'.

In the end I stayed on with Johnny till the end of the tour.

We went back to London returning to the Reteys' basement, as we had nowhere to live – that familiar refrain!

Johnny was very good with their little daughter Rosalind
and taught her to say, 'She's a good old woman but she will
be talking' which amused her. But when I visited them after
Johnny had died she never mentioned him. It was as if she'd
shut her mind to it.

Johnny was given a part in a children's TV series playing
Joe the milkman.

Oscar Lewenstein was now the manager at The Royal
Court Theatre. He asked me to cover Jean Forbes Robertson
(who had a drinking problem) as Branwen in *The Long
Mirror* by J.B. Priestly. I was to wait until curtain up then
leave, unbeknownst to the cast, once the performance had
started. I was leaving the theatre two days later after rehearsing the first two acts, when I met her at the stage door. 'Niver
work in the Wist Ind' she announced to me in a sarcastic
voice. I saw that she was inebriated and stayed on, hidden
from sight, up in the flies. After muddling her first lines in the
play the curtain was brought down. They were in a panic
down below, thinking I'd already left, when I appeared out of
nowhere. Within ten minutes I was on stage, made up, wearing my own clothes, not having rehearsed the third act, which
I made up as I went along. As you'll expect by now, a critic
wrote that, at very short notice I gave a performance that was
nothing short of brilliance. Mary Jerrold, an old actress in the
play, asked, 'Can't she take over?' but, wait for it, nothing happened. I continued as the secret cover.

Johnny was saved from playing Joe the milkman by being
asked to go for an interview with a young Michael Codron,

the producer. For some reason I went with him. I'd never done it before. Codron said, 'We must see if we can find something for you', but no more was said and Johnny started rehearsals.

Chapter Nineteen

I went back to Ipswich when Johnny's pre-London tour started, as I'd promised Rosebud that I'd do her temporary Christmas job instead of her in Footman Pretty and Co., selling rubber moulds. She couldn't do it as she was to sing in the wings for a touring ice-show. I was to be demonstrating, showing children how to make models from the moulds by filling them with a white liquid plaster, which hardened into the shape of a little animal. I remember on Saturday afternoons I sold a lot of these. I would double my sales every week because I took an interest in the children, made models for them to take home and paint and bring back to me and I would glaze them. So, of course, they would persuade their mothers to buy the set of moulds. It wasn't quite like the market in Surrey Street, Croydon (where I was to move when I had my children), where the banana seller would shout out,

'Cry baby, cry; make mother buy', but it was, unwittingly, the same idea.

Sometimes on Saturday afternoons it would all get too much, as I would be surrounded by all these little faces. I would duck down behind my stand to hide, just for a moment as I didn't want people looking at me any more – and then I'd bounce up and carry on.

Johnny came home for Christmas, and he wanted me to go back with him to Cardiff. Most affairs started in Cardiff because there was nothing much to do there then. I started one with an actor in Cardiff once myself.

I was really too tired to go. I'd worked very hard doing the selling job. It was Christmas Day and somehow I just couldn't get ready in time to go back with him on Boxing Day. I'd finished work late on Christmas Eve, my clothes weren't ready and it was all too much for me to drive the next morning all the way from Ipswich to Wales. So I didn't go (if I had gone things wouldn't have happened as they did). I didn't stay understanding for long because I was suddenly hit by a tremendous sense of loss; he had adored me, and everybody used to say, 'He wouldn't be anything without June.' And suddenly he was.

I'd bought myself a pair of shoes and a moleskin coat in Ipswich from my salary there. I'd lived in other peoples cast offs for several years. I didn't want to look shabby any more, by saving his money for him, not when she had joined us as we walked together down the platform as I'd been up to be with him for the Sunday in the middle of the tour. She, all in black; a long black coat with stylish flower-pot hat, shoes and a long umbrella to match. Me, in a second hand green herringbone coat with red medium heel court shoes that were too big for me. I'd felt badly dressed then and she hadn't deigned to answer me although I'd spoken to her. I thought, 'What an unfriendly girl', no more than that.

I was completely unaware that she found him attractive but I can see now why she behaved as she did to me.

I kissed him goodbye, waved as the train pulled out and went back to Ipswich to wash my clothes and pack my travel bag ready to join him in Bournemouth for their last week. I don't know why it didn't have a London run. I didn't hear from him. His usual letters didn't arrive.

Johnny told me about the affair, I didn't have to discover it.

I was delightfully kind and understanding. I'd been puzzled by his phone call from Kettering and now he looked so nerve-wracked.

'What's the matter?' I said and he told me. I think the only time I was angry was when he said half jokingly that she was going to be a dame and he was going to be a knight! I just seized a fold in his stomach and twisted it, and I wasn't a violent person.

His friend Georgie Rose was away, so he left me in Ipswich and went to live in Georgie's flat in Lymington Road in West Hampstead, I stayed at home and started to look for work, which had drifted away from me. There had been parts offered that I could have played and which would have been very good for me to do – Antigone, for instance – but I hadn't accepted them because Johnny always wanted me to be with him.

Ironically, he was afraid that I would meet someone else

and leave him. I have this theory that it's always the person who loves the most who is most likely to have an affair, as they're afraid that they will be abandoned. They don't feel secure in the love of the person they have. So if they meet someone, as he did with Maggie W, who they think they can trust more, they will be the one who leaves before being left. I can understand it, but it was painful for me at the time. She had made it obvious that she thought he was very attractive, she was confident, a much-loved only child of moneyed parents. A very witty, funny person and he was a very witty, funny man; I was not a witty girl.

I was quite witty before I married him. I think I 'dwindled into a wife', as Millamant says in Congreve's *The Way of the World* – 'I think I may, by degrees, dwindle into a wife.' And Mirabell responds, 'I may by degrees enlarge into a husband.'

Johnny was so much the centre of any gathering that I would sit and laugh with the others at his comments, and prompt his stories.

It was a very unhappy time, a very bleak time. For six weeks I couldn't eat, I couldn't sleep, I couldn't concentrate on anything. I couldn't go to see a film, I couldn't read a book – me, an avid reader. I used to go to church; I used to pray. I took sleeping pills in order to sleep.

Desperate for work, I went to see Glen Byam Shaw, who was by then the Artistic Director of the Stratford Memorial Company (now the Royal Shakespeare). He told me that he was to take a company on tour in this country and on the Continent and he would see what he could do for me.

Then I told him why and poured all my angst out to him.

I left Glen's office and in the street outside I made a call to Johnny from a phone box. When he answered I said, 'Hello.'

'Is that you Maggie?' He sounded amused.

'No, it's not Maggie'.

I went to Lymington Road, either it was or had been the day before my twenty-eighth birthday. Johnny gave me a pair of stockings. I took size ten, these were nine and a half. 'They're the wrong size – give them to somebody else.'

As I removed my coat he looked at me, 'You're so thin', he said.

Always before he'd given me the lilies-of-the-valley, out of season, a gift carefully chosen and wrapped, a manicure set, a pair of black leather gauntlets.

Deeply depressed I returned two or three days later. On learning that Agnes, my cousin John's wife, had had her first baby, I drove Auntie Lottie up to Loughborough to help after the birth. The weather was so cold but there was no heater in my Morris Series E, so Uncle Billy had wrapped Auntie Lottie up in brown paper and newspaper to keep her warm.

At one point, I skidded the car, and all I said was 'Oo-er!' In an emergency I am usually very calm. But we got there safely, and I found great comfort because I was very fond of my cousin. In the fortnight I spent with them we talked a lot to each other, as we had when we were childhood companions.

I had to get a job to support myself. I had no husband, no friend in him any more, no home, no laughter, no career and no money.

Wallace Everett gave me an audition to play Kate in Shakespeare's *The Taming of the Shrew*. I'd done *Time and the Conways* with him there and he said, 'What's happened to your lovely voice?' I had had a very rich, warm, attractive voice, but the pain in it made it sound harsh and cracked.

1949 Colchester Repertory – July 4th–9th – Time And The Conways.

June Brown, one of the four newcomers in this performance, is brilliant as the sensitive Kay Conway, being, if it is possible, outstanding in a first-rate cast.

But this time my voice wasn't an advantage to me. I didn't get the job.

I rang Johnny to ask if I could join him in George's flat so that I could look for work in London and I had friends there and I was hoping his affair might have come to attend. He was rehearsing Old Gobbo in *The Merchant* for the BBC.

I went to pick him up from rehearsal at the end of the day and realised they'd ended much earlier than I'd imagined. When we got home I questioned him and he admitted to me that he had a key to Maggie's flat, which was further down the Finchley Road, very close to George's flat and that he'd been going there while she was away on a pre-London tour for another play and there he'd been writing letters and receiving them from her.

I was distraught. I'd hoped the affair was over. I found myself standing on the sofa facing the wall with my arms outstretched, not knowing what to do, where to go, what to say. The next morning I decided I had to leave Johnny. I couldn't bear anymore.

I went to see Rosie hoping that Leighton was away and I could stay there but found he'd just come back from his tour. She was just about to go to the dental surgery where she had a temporary job so said she'd ask her friend there, Maureen, if I could stay with her, knowing that she had a flat just off the Finchley Road. Maureen said she'd take me in. She was very kind to me. When you're in that state all you want to do is talk about it over and over again and she was a quiet, patient listener.

After three days I went to get the rest of my clothes, thinking that Johnny would be at rehearsals and found that he was there in the flat. We didn't talk, I just gathered up the rest of my clothes. Upon going I told him I was leaving him and walked out.

Walking back to Maureen's flat having made my decision I felt free, quite calm, no longer obsessed. When I was almost there I saw a rather appealing-looking dog who made me smile; I bent down and stroked him and became conscious of the fact that Johnny had been following me. He came into the flat with me. He would be doing his dress rehearsal that afternoon and he was agitated. It was not to do with the rehearsal, he was upset about what had happened to us and he told me what had happened between them and what they had done. He had been to see a solicitor to find out if he could divorce me for that one stupid afternoon I'd spent with that actor at the Mercury Theatre so that I would be the guilty party as the divorce laws stood and she'd be left out of it. It would upset her parents she'd told him. When I was travelling back to London, he'd hoped I'd throw myself off the train and they had lived together that last week in Bournemouth but he hadn't made love to her, not fully because she was a virgin.

I was shattered.

He came towards me to put his arms around me.

I drew away from him, 'Don't touch me! Don't come near me'.

By this time we were both very upset and because he had to do his dress rehearsal I told him to lie down on my bed while I got him some food. I went back with him so that he would be calm enough to be able to rehearse.

Just as I was due to start my own rehearsals, George Devine, who was very fond of Johnny, rang to ask him to take over the parts of an actor already cast whom he'd dropped from the company.

George had been informed that this actor wouldn't be available for a fortnight due to another engagement – George wasn't pleased and invited Johnny to take his place. It was very fortunate for us, it solved our problem as it meant we'd be together and out of the country.

Johnny wrote Maggie his last letter. I did not ask to see it. He was to say two years afterwards, 'I ruined our marriage.'

I made friends on that tour as a safe-guard so that he wasn't my sole support and I wouldn't feel left again in isolation.

That September 1955, we started the European tour headed by Sir John Gielgud, Peggy Ashcroft, not yet a dame, and George Devine. There were too many in the company for me to list but Judith Stott and her husband Jeremy Burnham were to becoming amusing and supportive friends of mine.

Judith and I played pageboys in *Lear* dressed in tights joined to tunics with balaclavas on our heads and a wig on top.

The costumes and sets for this *Lear* were by Noguchi, a Japanese designer, and were absolutely frightful. They were avant-garde and what the meaning was behind them, none of us could fathom. Our tights were brown on one side and black on the other and vice versa.

In order to go to the loo we had to remove the wig over the balaclava, which was attached to the top of the tunic and pull down the whole costume. This could be a very cold experience in the winter.

What the Germans, Austrians, Danes, Swedes and Norwegians thought of the production I don't know as I couldn't read their press notices.

Poor Sir John was desolate, very unhappy. He had been enjoying the rehearsals, even when George Devine had given him a note not to be so poetic but more down-to-earth. His answer to that was, 'Oh, I see what you mean, George, less suede shoes and more Roger Livesey.'

I fear that I will have to explain why we found it very amusing. Suede shoes were the prerogative of gay men and Roger Livesey a very masculine actor. Now, if I repeat it, will you laugh?

However much we laughed about it, Sir John was not amused. The clothes made him feel distinctly unregal, awkward and embarrassed. He was so uncomfortable in them, and although he felt that they were destroying his beautifully spoken King Lear he only moaned about them to us, the actors, and made no demur about wearing them. He was a very humble dear man, friendly to everyone. Theatre discipline was tight in those days, you did as you were told.

Even his throne become a tip-tilted golden lavatory seat with a large oval hole cut in the middle. His clothes got less and less as the play went on until he was almost naked. I think I see what Noguchi was up to now but the reduction of Lear's power is told in the wonderful words and in the action. It really doesn't need underlining in such an obvious way. I can hear Gielgud as Lear talking to his dead daughter, Cordelia, to this day, 'We two will sing like birds'.

He did sing his words in a way, something he was often accused of, but he was a delight to listen to.

I'd rather see him perform than any Johnny-one-note actor. He was so moving with that last speech, covered as he was, at least, by a robe. Or could it have been a dressing gown, symbol of his approaching long sleep, his death.

Judith wore her jewellery with her costume, gold earrings and many rings and she kept her suspender belt on as well. There was an outline of the knobs, holding up her stockings underneath her leggings, nobody seemed to notice. We were invited on to a boat in Copenhagen for some party and Judith, who hadn't eaten, was rather woozy when we disembarked and headed off to the theatre. I kept a close eye on her on stage, surreptitiously edging half a step sideways in order, if necessity arose, to throw my arm around her and march us both off into the wings. She managed to keep upright.

In Berlin, Johnny and I would take advantage of the very well-known hotel, Kempinski, that we were staying in to have a very late enormous breakfast to avoid buying lunch. It was a pleasure to eat with a tall glass of freshly squeezed orange juice, which was unusual in England, beautifully cooked bacon and eggs and real coffee now known to us through the many coffee bars that had sprung up during the Fifties in London.

In fact, when we were performing at the Palace Theatre for a few weeks afterwards, Judith and I would slip out of the stage door and into Old Compton Street to while away an hour or so during the performance. I should not have gone as I was understudying Goneril and would have been missing if she fainted or twisted her ankle. 'Come on my darling, we can't sit in that boring old theatre all night,' said my temptress, and that's what we did every night.

Johnny didn't come out with us as he was playing Oswald, so I spent a lot of time with Judith.

He got up to his usual mischievous behaviour in Amsterdam. One night we were walking along one of the canal streets and he was amused by the continuous line of bicycles all chained to the railings, and he was seized by the desire to let the air out of the tyres. The other young male actors latched on with glee, there they all were laughing away. I thought how awful it would be in the morning when their owners arrived to go to work and would be maniacally pumping away, their arms going up and down like pistons. Johnny saw it in a different light, imagining how funny that scene would be. Oh dear, he was always playing tricks just to amuse himself.

Peggy was not going to play Cordelia, not in London, she said, 'At fifty I'm too told.' Claire Bloom would take over for her and was rehearsing with us in Amsterdam. She was a very friendly girl in spite of becoming a film star when Charles

Chaplin chose her to be in *Limelight* with him and she often came out with our rabble. She almost tripped over a jutting-out step on one of the canal streets in Amsterdam, 'Be careful, Clara, you nearly went for a Burton.' I was looked at by the others as if they thought I didn't realise what I'd said. Claire had a passion for Richard Burton. Of course I'd said it on purpose. I couldn't resist. She ignored it.

Then there was Harold Lang, who became a friend of ours. He was a very talkative and inventive chap, constantly assuming the persona of Naomi Jacobs, the writer whom Harold called the lesbian novelist. He filled in an entry card on the plane once stating his name as Miss Naomi Jacobs and his occupation lesbian novelist.

We were on the train going to Zurich when we passed a field of very small fir trees, 'One of my plantations,' he remarked. He always played Naomi Jacobs with a northern accent, we knew he was referring to dildos and we were laughing at him. Sir John asked what we were laughing at. Harold tried to explain but without success. Sir John just looked bemused.

So anyway, I poured everything out about Johnny and the affair, how I'd more or less given up the theatre for him, how I'd devoted myself to him, to our life together . . . and he gave me a job in the company as understudy and walk-on. In other words, I started again at the bottom of the ladder. A long time afterwards Glen said to me, 'You'll never guess who was in the room next door when you were telling me all about Johnny!' I couldn't guess and I still don't know, but I've often wondered whether it was Maggie W.

I didn't really want to go away from him then, and be in this company without him, but coincidentally one of the actors wasn't going to be available until the middle of rehearsals, so suddenly Johnny was in the company, too.

The following year, Tony Quayle asked Johnny and me if we would join the Stratford company for a year. George Devine had already asked Johnny to join the company he was starting at the Royal Court, but there was no definite date. It was one of those casual things where George had said to him, 'You'll come with me, won't you, to my company at the Royal Court?' And Johnny had said yes; but as the bird in the hand is worth two in the bush, he accepted Tony Quayle's offer, too. Unfortunately Tony mentioned to Johnny, in front of George, how happy he was that Johnny would be in his company.

Had he gone to the Royal Court with George Devine he would have played the Alan Bates part in *Look Back in Anger*. Sometimes that's just the way life goes. You take the wrong path . . .

Because of Johnny's affair, I suppose I learnt never to put all my eggs in one basket again. I lost my trust. So this time, I made a lot of friends on the tour, particularly Judith Stott, who was married to Jeremy Burnham at the time. Now I had another support rather than just the one person. I was twenty-eight years old.

Oscar Lewenstein once said to me about Johnny and me, 'You two are like two guns propped together – take one away and the other will fall down.' And I think that maybe Johnny *should* have gone to Maggie. Maybe that would have been the right thing to do, and perhaps then he would have become a knight and she a dame.

I think the reason he had started the affair was because I'd had a brief fling, nothing very great. When you're acting that you're in love with someone, it's very hard not to think you are. I was doing a play at the Mercury Theatre, which was in Notting Hill Gate. This chap who was playing opposite me – well, we had a sort of one-afternoon fling. I regretted it immediately. I felt quite dirty afterwards and went home and got in the bath, trying to wash it all away, and I was fool enough to tell Johnny. I must have felt guilty, I suppose. I don't know why, I can't remember now how it came up.

He got into a terrible state and opened the window and was going to jump out. We were living in Holly Hill in Peter Copley's house at the time. I remember grabbing him and holding him to stop him from jumping.

And he said to me afterwards that he'd be better off married to a cross between a restaurant and a Chinese laundry!

We were in the middle of this terrible row, and I just started to laugh because it was so true. I wasn't very good at washing and ironing – we didn't have washing machines, everything had to be done by hand then, of course, everything had to be ironed and there were no easy-care fabrics like there are now. And 'married to a restaurant' was just so funny because the food I cooked was never ready – certainly not everything at the same time.

Chapter Twenty

It was the first flat that we ever rented on our own, the one where he killed himself – 6 Elsham Road, West Kensington. I've never liked the number six since.

I was buying a new car recently and signed the papers, then realised the registration numbers added up to the number six. So, I took the car back and exchanged it. I just didn't feel comfortable driving around with an 'unlucky' number plate.

Well, quite honestly, the day he died I was going to spend the night at Rosie's flat – I've never told anybody this but I was completely exhausted. Rosebud was living in Artesian Road, about a ten-minute drive away with her husband Leighton who was in a musical play in the West End, and her baby son Martin.

I'd had no sleep with Johnny for so long.

Then Johnny developed a condition of the mouth called lichen vulgaris, which is like thrush. His teeth and gums were infected. He had very nice teeth and he became very fussy about them, flossing them all the time, and every time he ate anything he cleaned them in order to keep the infection at bay. I remember he went to Guy's Hospital or St Thomas's to be seen by a specialist, and there were students standing around. The specialist said, 'It isn't a very important or serious condition.' Johnny retorted, 'It's all very well for you, you haven't got moss in the mouth!' Which caused the students to all fall about laughing.

He retained this sense of humour, despite the depression. He always got very depressed at certain times, particularly when he was out of work.

When he was a student at RADA, one of the other students, Richard Pascoe, told me Johnny was light hearted, nothing worried him, he was full of joy and laughter. He never worked outside RADA, he only worked when he was there, and he won all the medals outright except the Gold. He was expected to win this as well. The only reason he didn't was because his father had become agitated, really worried that Johnny would be called up to fight in the Second World War.

His father Wilfred had volunteered as a sixteen-year-old in the First World War, but when he got to the trenches he couldn't bear the horror of it all. He was injured in his neck from a shell fragment and invalided home. He decided to act as if he was shell-shocked, because he couldn't face going back to the trenches. He developed Ménière's disease in which the nerves in the ears atrophy, and he became stone deaf.

Although he was able to reply to you verbally, you had to write everything down for him. He was a witty clever man who had won a scholarship to Uppingham at the age of fourteen but left at sixteen because he was a scholarship boy and from a poor background. He couldn't stand being amongst the other, privileged boys. His mind was far, far above any of those of his family or the people where he lived. He was employed as a shipping clerk. When he left, they had to get three men to replace him in the job he had been doing for £2.75 a week.

Wilfred was an only child for seven years then two more children were born in quick succession. He was exceedingly jealous of them and they were terrified of him.

He was always studying and they weren't allowed to make a noise – they used to flee to the next door neighbours house to hide from him. When Wilfred finally married he didn't want any children. He wanted to be the centre of attention. So, when Johnny was conceived it was through a hole in a washable rubber sheath which his wife Theresa had secretly cut. He was exceedingly unpleasant to Theresa while she was pregnant.

The baby was born with a caul over his face after a very difficult birth on 31 October. I remember his mother saying what agony the birth was but when the baby was born and they took the caul off, there was this beautiful little face. Which reminds me of when my daughter Sophie was born. She had her arm wrapped round her face so when she came out she didn't look like a newborn baby, all stretched from the pressure, but like a beautiful little girl. In fact, my brother-in-law Leighton said she was the most

beautiful newborn baby he'd ever seen. It wasn't very pleasant for me. 'This one's got a big head,' I said, which she
hadn't at all.

Anyway, back to Johnny. It was only once Johnny was born
that his father suddenly took an enormous interest in him.
His mother discovered that he had a talent for acting, and
from then on he was encouraged by both parents to be a
great actor. His middle name was Gascoigne. He would be a
knight, he had the name for it already, 'John Gascoigne
Garley'!

His mother doted on him but she doted on him in the
right sort of way. For instance, she disciplined him. He found
his mother very funny. Her cooking was not very good but
Johnny praised it to the skies and there was always a twinkle
in his eye. He used to say to her, 'You're a good old trout.' She
had a most hysterical sort of laugh; lots of people found it
very amusing – I didn't, quite honestly – but it was a laugh
that everybody knew and laughed about and it became
rather notorious, a very high-pitched cackle. She adored
Johnny and he made her laugh; he was the light of her life.

His father, this very clever, creative man, wrote adapta-
tions of *A Christmas Carol* for him before Emlyn Williams
thought of it. His father did the same with *Love on the Dole* –
when Johnny performed this he was approached by the
Labour Party and asked whether he would be a candidate for
them. Johnny had no interest in politics whatsoever, except
that he adored Winston Churchill whom he could impersonate better than any person I have ever heard. He was a
brilliant impersonator.

He'd get letters from his father saying, '<u>You must get</u>

deferment', 'You must get deferment'. Wilfred had become obsessed with the idea that Johnny must not have his career destroyed. As I said earlier, he became very, very worried as the time for Johnny's call-up came near. He kept saying, 'You're a good actor, say that all the bombs and landmines in London have affected you and that you have neurasthenia. You must get deferment. Johnny wasn't at all concerned about the air raids. When the sirens sounded he just used to get into bed and go to sleep.

His father was an extremely important influence on him; he would have him walking round the garden with books on his head for his posture, making him rehearse his solo recitals every moment of his spare time. When Johnny was a student at RADA, he went home one weekend and his father persuaded him to act up. 'You can do it,' he said to him. 'You're a clever actor. Pretend your nerves have gone because of the bombing.' But Johnny wanted to join the Air Force and his mother would say, 'Leave the boy alone, let him go into the Air Force.'

Wilfred was anxious that this son, in whom he'd invested all his hopes, would do what he himself had never done – make a name for himself, be successful. So Johnny, because he loved and was influenced by his father, did as he wanted; when he had his interview before his call-up and he acted as though his nerves had been shot to pieces and subsequently was graded C3.

The next time he went home, his father said to him, 'Did you do it?' and Johnny's reply was, 'Yes.'

To which Wilfred immediately said, 'We'll be found out, prosecuted! We'll be at the Old Bailey!'

And from then on, his father did nothing but worry, drink tea and smoke cigarettes.

When Johnny saw him in that state he said to him, 'If you're not careful, you'll land up in Berrywood!', which was the local mental asylum. His father looked at him and he said, 'Do you know, I think you're right?' Johnny told me he'd never forget his father's look. Johnny felt that he saw this as the solution to the problem.

If he had not been 'in his right mind' at the time, he could not be found guilty of persuading his son to deceive the authorities. From that moment, Wilfred started acting as if he were suffering from schizophrenia; he said he heard voices, the Germans were wiring the lawn, he was being watched. After a few weeks of this, Johnny's mother was so exhausted that she took Wilfred to his father and asked him to have his son for the night.

'He's your husband – you look after him,' she was told. 'Yes, and he's your son!'

Eventually, he went voluntarily into a psychiatric hospital. Unfortunately, at the end of his short stay there a police car followed them the whole way home. He had become like the officer in *Colditz* who acted out having a nervous breakdown, then, when released, never came out of the psychiatric condition. I think that's what happened to Wilfred.

When they finally took him back to the hospital, he was certified. As he went through the gates he said, 'At last, I'm in the right place.' And he never came out again. He was not dangerous, he never threatened anybody, he never hurt anybody but from the age of about fifty he lived in a psychiatric hospital until he died.

The strange thing was that when I married Johnny, his mother, Theresa, was always talking about Wilfred and saying, 'Won't it be lovely when your dad comes home?' and I thought she really meant it. All the time I'd known her, that had been her whole dream. So I, innocently, did all I could to get him out. When she realised there was a possibility of it actually happening, she went completely haywire, 'Oh, I couldn't have him here, I couldn't. I couldn't live with him. I couldn't.'

She was a dutiful wife all the same. She visited him once a fortnight, wrote to him. But she didn't really want him back.

I had become so incensed with the people running the mental home – the atrocious conditions where the patients had hardly any space between the beds, the very deeply deranged were kept alongside people who were only slightly disturbed; patients were kept on Haloperidol, had to eat with their fingers – that I wrote to the Board of Control.

They did a spot check and the superintendent was removed.

I had energy in those days. I was twenty-five.

We moved Wilfred to Virginia Water, where there was a private hospital and managed to get him a bed for £2 a week. Although it doesn't sound very much, I was earning £10 a week and sending money to Rosebud to help her through her college, so it was quite a lot.

Wilfred didn't really like it in the south; he preferred Northamptonshire where he was born and bred, and had never left, except to go to the trenches in France.

A few years later these cost nothing because he was working – he looked after other patients, he cleaned, he did everything. He stayed in Virginia Water then, and he died there.

Once Johnny had been passed C3 for the services, which is a very low rating, he was chosen in a random ballot to be a Bevin Boy. It was just the luck of the draw – they picked you out of a hat, more or less, and you went down the mines.

There were all sorts – doctors' sons, builders, all classes, shapes and sizes, but when Johnny arrived at the mine he found that he suffered from claustrophobia. It could possibly have been because he was born with a caul over his face – I don't know, but I would imagine it was to do with his birth.

He was absolutely terrified of going underground. I remember that if we were in the Tube and it stopped in the tunnel his face would go white and he would go absolutely rigid. He was terrified of being underground in this hole, not moving.

And it was something I can't understand because I am not frightened of tunnels; I'm not frightened of heights. I'm only frightened of the supernatural.

When he discovered he had claustrophobia, he acted as if he was having a nervous breakdown so as to get out. His doctor, Dr Emmanuel, who was a German Jew and had got out of Germany before the war, was terribly patient with him. He used to come in every day to read with him to help him regain his voice. Johnny was acting all the time – he was perfectly all right. When he heard them talking about shock treatment, he very rapidly got better.

Looking back, I think it was very funny. If he could have told me now, I would have laughed. But when he did finally come to confess all this to me, I was pulled into his misery and guilt so that I couldn't stay light-hearted. I thought it was dreadful, too.

When we were in Stratford, Andrew Faulds, a very socialist chap at the time of the Suez Crisis in 1956, got Johnny into a terrible state, feeling that he was responsible for Suez and that he ought to go and dig ditches and repair the country. I don't think Andrew ever did this himself. But Johnny, by this time, was in quite a sensitive state. Guilt acted like a whirlpool within him; it was slow to begin with, but got rapidly worse when he was out of work and when he came back from seeing his father. And it was after he had given up on that job in Nottingham that he said to me, 'Never let me give up again, never.'

We had both been offered a job at Nottingham – so he could have been working. He was supposed to have played the servant Truffaldino in the *Servant of Two Masters* by Goldoni. He'd got into this state of mind of wanting to give up, and I tried to persuade him to play the part because I think you should never give up. Once you give up, it's the start of the end. But he didn't take any notice of me. I spent my time trying, but he wouldn't do it, so he was on his own in the digs while I was playing for a month in *The Merchant of Yonkers* and as Beatrice, one of the masters in the *Servant of Two Masters*. Then when we went back to London he began to be very worried and used to talk in half-sentences, and I would answer the first half in a straightforward way. We were living in Elsham Road when he was offered a TV play called *The Survivors* and was in the middle of rehearsals, and a week later I was to start a television play called *The*

Case of the Frightened Lady. I did start rehearsals the day after his funeral. He was frightened that he'd got VD, so he went to St Mary's, Paddington. He said later, 'You didn't come with me', but I didn't even know he'd been there. He hadn't got VD. Then he told me that he'd had one one-night-stand when he was in Ireland and felt terribly guilty about it, and that was the reason he thought constantly that he had VD.

To fill the gap left when a larger-than-life person is taken from you, in whatever way, is almost impossible, and it can remain empty for a long time. Thoughts about them come into your head most unexpectedly and bring with them the remembrance of their humour, their laughter.

The day before Johnny committed suicide, he'd bought a will form and taken a breadknife out of the drawer, and pretended to threaten me with it. All I did was open the front door and push him out on to the landing. He was in his pyjamas, and within seconds he was saying, 'Let me in, let me in!' He was trying to prove to himself that he was mad. He was afraid that he was going mad. He wasn't. He was completely and utterly sane.

Georgie Rose had told him to see his doctor, and apparently the doctor had said to Georgie afterwards, 'Well, I hope he has a breakdown soon because he's driving his wife to distraction.'

The strange part was that I wasn't aware that I was on this kind of knife edge. But I do remember going to get some cigarettes from the pub on the corner of Elsham Road and as I walked past on the other side from our flat a dog leapt out and barked at me; when I told the landlady she said, 'That's very funny, he never does that.' I think the dog sensed my state of high nervous tension.

I was hopeful his depressions would lift now that he had *The Survivors* and he was working. I was hopeful life would be easier for us, but it wasn't to be so. Johnny still couldn't sleep. I was exhausted. 'I can't have this all my life,' he would say, referring to the lichen. I tried to reassure him, not knowing that, for him, there was an underlying reason why he felt he would be forced to suffer it for ever. Never having smoked, he tried one of my cigarettes in the hope that it might calm him down, but only the one.

He was given no medication. He made another appointment with the local doctor, who was going to give him hypnosis. I was unaware of this, as he was keeping so much from me. It was to prove too late for him. He would not be keeping the appointment.

The night before he died, he made what was to all intents and purposes his confession. 'I feel so guilty,' he told me. 'It's my fault – it's because of me that Dad's in that mental home. He's been stuck in there for thirteen years and there's no end in sight, no hope of him ever coming out. I know he wouldn't be in that place if I hadn't written that note telling him, "If you go on like this, you'll end up in Berrywood." Dad read it, looked straight at me and said, "I think you're right." So you see, it was me – I put the idea in his head. Then he started acting being mad. I think he thought, if he was put in the asylum, he wouldn't be responsible for his actions and they couldn't prosecute him if they found out that he'd made me pretend to have neurasthenia to get deferment. So it's all my fault he is in there.

'And when I was taken down that mine, I realised that I had claustrophobia. I was panic-stricken in the dark and I could hardly breathe. I had to get out. So I pretended I had hit my head and it made me stutter. So I was discharged. Then I had to see Dr Emmanuel and I had to keep stammering.

'He was completely taken in. He used to come every day to read with me, hoping he could help me get rid of it. It was only when I heard him and Ma talking on the landing about giving me electric shock treatment, that I thought I'd better pretend to get better.

'I feel so guilty because Dr Emmanuel still believes that he cured me. He didn't because I was acting it and I should never have done it – used my acting the wrong way. It was a gift and I prostituted it and my poor mother was so distraught, what with Dad and then me, that she had a breakdown, too. And everything was my fault. I went to the Catholic church – the one along the road – and I saw a young priest and I asked him to hear my confession but he wouldn't. And the doctor said that I had to have this in my mouth all the time because if I didn't, I would go mad, so I don't know what to do. I'm so sorry. I'm so sorry.'

He had tried to be forgiven in the Catholic church just along Holland Road, but it was a young priest there and the reason he wouldn't hear his confession was because he wasn't a Catholic. Barry Keegan, who was an actor friend of his, said to me, 'It's a pity it wasn't an old priest – an old priest would have heard his confession.'

Then he managed to get through on the phone to a homeopathic doctor, Sharma Chandra, but somehow the little boy down below disconnected the call; we didn't have a private phone and we could only receive calls, not make them.

So it seemed as if everything went wrong and everything was coincidence.

I thought he would be all right because he'd confessed everything to me and he'd gradually start to get better. But he didn't, of course; it was like his final confession before he killed himself.

That last morning, he woke me up because he was afraid; he wanted to talk all the time. I remember hammering on his chest and saying, 'I must sleep. I must sleep!' He had bruises on his chest where I had hammered. He stood at the window and said, 'Isn't it a lovely day!' He went to rehearsal that morning and when he came home he said, 'They laughed today.' Even in the state he was in, in that play *The Survivors* he had made the other actors laugh. And, of course, it was they who were to be the survivors.

I've always said in the past that I left Johnny that day in order to do the ironing. My iron was broken – somebody had used it, dropped and broken it – and I had a lot of ironing to do. But I didn't. I wanted a night's sleep. I told Johnny I was going to stay with Rosebud that night. I'd never left him before without making him promise he wouldn't do anything foolish but this time I didn't make him promise it. So I left with my ironing and went to Rosie's.

Leighton had gone to a matinee – it was a Saturday. Rosie and I went for a walk along Queens Road with her son Martin. I remember saying to her, 'Isn't it marvellous to be free, not to have these husbands about, just us with Martin.'

We went and had a coffee in a little café and I bought a

bottle of wine and some food, we went back to Rosie's flat. I, suddenly, began to get extremely apprehensive.

I said to Rosie, 'I've got to go back and see how Johnny is.'

I got in the car and drove to Elsham Road and as I drew up I looked up at the front windows of our flat. The curtains were drawn. I knew that something awful had happened.

I ran upstairs to our top flat but the bedroom door was locked.

I ran back downstairs. The house was managed by an Irish couple, Mr and Mrs Seward. Mr Seward broke the door open and Johnny was lying in the bed in his pyjamas. He'd put his shoes neatly under the bed with his socks tucked into them – he was a very neat man – he'd put his money and his watch on the dressing table, his coat over the chair, his clothes folded and the gas fire was on the pillow beside his face. The windows were shut, the curtains were drawn and a suicide note was on the bed with his will written on a page of the script of *The Survivors*.

I remember throwing the gas fire on the floor, turning it off and Mr Seward and I dragged him out of the bed. He wasn't breathing, but I did artificial respiration for an hour until my blouse was damp. Mr Seward phoned for a doctor but it was Saturday afternoon and he couldn't contact one so, he called the ambulance.

Johnny began to breathe again, but I had damaged one of his kidneys with my artificial respiration and his brain was by then damaged by the gas. He had been dead for too long.

When the police came I lied to Sergeant Green – I said it must have been a gas leak.

*

Twenty or more years later, when she was fourteen, my daughter Sophie found the note and she cried. But it wasn't the real one – by now, the police had that. They'd sent me a copy. Johnny wrote his note on the back of a piece of script paper. I hid that and his will from the police sergeant who arrived on the scene.

JUNE MY DARLING LOVE,

I went to bed soon after you left and tried so hard to think as you have tried to show me. I am in great fear that all is lost. I love you so very, very dearly and I do hope and pray that you'll be able to forgive me. All I have (not much I fear) is yours my darling, please, please try to find some happiness for yourself.

I go with your dear sweet face there in front of me – in my mind's eye.

The world as I look out is very, very lovely and so are you. You'll find it hard to forgive I know but please – please, I beg it. I love you, I love you, I love you.

God bless you dear pussy face. All my fondest love for ever and ever,

John

WILL

I give and bequeath unto my wife June Muriel Garley, all that I possess, and to thank her for her kindness and devotion to me through-out this difficult time my dearest darling I love you so very much and pray that you will be happy in the future, as you so richly deserve. God bless you my love. Please try to forgive me, but I am so very tired.

Died Wednesday 8 May 1957 – Cremated at West
London Crematorium on 11 May 1957.

He'd got into bed, and he'd put that little gas fire beside him.

The doctors asked me if we had any drugs, any strychnine, in the flat, because he was very stiff when he was taken in. But I know why he was stiff : because he'd held himself there, forced himself to stay because he didn't want to do what he felt he had to do.

When I found him he had pinkish ears and a pink colour, but he looked perfectly normal to me. The police and ambulance came and took him to the West London Hospital, I went there in the police car with Sergeant Green and I talked all the time. They must know something's wrong – they say nothing and you just talk. I didn't talk about anything to do with the fact that he'd killed himself. I just talked.

I must have rung his mother because she arrived on the Monday with his uncle Jack and stayed at the hotel next door. It had happened on the Saturday, but I hadn't rung her till then, hoping he would recover. When Theresa arrived, the nurses had put me in a room to rest as I hadn't slept since Friday. Theresa was so upset that she woke me up. When she saw him her first words were, 'But his career'. Johnny was given oxygen to begin with, and they gave him oxygen at the end, but for the rest of the time in hospital he was just lying in bed.

I stayed at the hospital until Tuesday evening when Alan Badel arrived. How Alan found out where I was, I don't know, but suddenly he appeared round the curtain.

I was sitting by the bed, I'd got my face on the pillow

beside Johnny and he was lying there unconscious. Alan took me away. I hadn't slept, I hadn't had a bath. One of the nurses said to me, 'Was that Alan Badel? I saw his Romeo – he was wonderful!'

I told Alan that.

He took me back to his flat, he ran me a bath – and Vonnie gave me some food. They were the kindest of friends. I went to bed and thought, 'I shall never sleep.' But I did. I had asked Alan to wake me if the hospital rang and he'd said he would. At about 6 o'clock I had vaguely heard the phone ring. It was the phone call to tell me that Johnny was dying.

I didn't get there in time but his mother was with him – she gave him life and she was there when he died; in a way I feel that that was fitting. She was never the same again. All her laughter went.

That night that Johnny died, I woke up suddenly and I knew exactly why he had killed himself. I realised that he'd been terrified of going mad. The lichen vulgaris in his mouth was a terrible trouble to him, causing a constant stinging sensation.

He'd been to see the doctor who'd told him that he had the choice of either facing the prospect of the lichen all his life, or going mad. I suddenly realised what all those half-sentences had meant when he used to say to me, 'But I can't have this all my life, can I'.

Alan took me to the hospital the next day, the mortuary where he identified Johnny for me, as I wasn't there when he died – and then to the undertakers to arrange his funeral. I drove myself to the police station – Sergeant Green, who'd come to our flat when the ambulance was called, took me to see the coroner. We sat down with him, and the first thing I said was, 'I'm afraid I wasn't telling the truth.' Sergeant Green got up hastily and said, 'Excuse me, I have to go' and quickly left the room because I'd deceived the police which was a crime. He very kindly didn't want to have to charge me – so he avoided my confession.

I explained to the coroner that Johnny had thought that he was going mad, that he wasn't and I really didn't want a verdict of 'suicide while of unsound mind' to be brought in, because that would confirm Johnny's worst fears. In the end, the verdict was simply that he 'killed himself' – an unusual verdict in those days.

Actually, he did regain consciousness at one point. The doctor had said to me, 'If he recovers, he could be incontinent, incapable, but he will know what he has done.' I was saying, 'If he recovers, he will be fine; if he does not then he will die.' I suppose I was saying, 'Don't let him live if he's going to be like that.' I was sitting there – I think it was the very day that Alan came to the hospital and took me off to get some sleep – and Johnny was in his unconscious state and I was talking to him and he opened his eyes and said, 'Darling, hello.' Then his face seemed to tense up and I said, 'Calm down, it's all right', and he slipped back out of consciousness and never regained it.

But they didn't believe me.

At the coroner's court, the coroner asked me, 'Did he regain consciousness?' and I looked at the doctor and I said, 'I thought so, yes. He said to me, "Darling, hello."'

When I listened to what the doctor said had been found out at the post mortem, that he had got a damaged kidney, I knew I'd done it – it must have been my constant pushing down on his body when I was trying to resuscitate him. I'd used the sort of artificial respiration I'd been taught as a girl at high school when I got my bronze medallion for lifesaving. I knelt beside him and put my hands on his lower back, then leant my weight on them.

I swung on to them and swung back and swung on to them, then swung back and so on. I probably used too much pressure and I damaged it that way. I did get him breathing again but he would have been brain damaged.

That night Alan and Yvonne said, 'Let's go to the pictures.'

I said, 'No. I have to tell people that Johnny has died.'

I phoned a few people from their flat but then went out to the phone box in the foyer of the block of flats.

I didn't want to use their phone to keep saying the same thing – 'I've got some rather dreadful news. Sit down. Have you got a drink?'

I didn't break at any point. In the phone box I saw on the wall a drawing of what looked like an oxygen mask – it looked almost like a gas mask and I couldn't stay there, so I left.

I walked up Hanger Lane to a phone box on the hill; and while I was in there I felt a hand touch my shoulder.

I had talked to several people before this, and the only person I cried to was Georgie Rose after this happened because I was terrified, I'd seen that oxygen mask and something had touched me.

I hurried back to the flat. That morning as I walked in to their sitting room I had heard someone call my name. I turned round to Yvonne and said, 'Yes?'

But she just looked at me. 'I didn't say anything.'

Then I said, 'I heard someone call my name.'

'Oh, it must be the children in that school over there.'

But I am still sure it wasn't the children – the voice was from inside the room.

The night before they had let me sleep in their bed and that was when I thought I wouldn't sleep. I was terrified of the supernatural; I was terrified of seeing Johnny.

But I did sleep, and actually it was in the morning that I knew exactly what had happened – it was as if everything was crystal-clear. I knew exactly why he'd killed himself and how he had felt and the state of mind he had been in, and the terrible fear. It was as if he had pushed me into acknowledging that fear: 'That's what *you're* frightened of, Junie' and this was what *I* was frightened of. I told Yvonne, who was marvellous – I dragged her out of bed at six o'clock in the morning and poured it all out. She was wonderful.

When I talked to Alan, he was marvellous too, because I felt a lot of guilt and Alan only asked me questions. 'Why do you say it?' – 'Why do you think he did that?' Then he would let me talk about it myself. He was the most marvellous comfort and support, and so was Vonnie.

After Johnny's death Ollie, Pam's husband, bumped into me in Ipswich one day and said jokingly, 'Where's your husband, has he run off with another woman?' and I said, 'No, he's died' and his attitude changed immediately. I have

always wondered why one gets more sympathy and understanding when you lose a partner through death rather than
to another person, which I think far, far, harder to suffer.

I went down to my parents. I didn't phone them. I took half
a bottle of brandy with me. I told my mother what had happened.

My father was in bed recovering from a stroke; he'd just
got a job, and thinking he was still young jumped off the
trolleybus as it came past our house, slowing down to go
round the corner. He stumbled and fell and never worked
again because the shock of it was too much.

I didn't tell him that Johnny was dead because he was
very, very fond of him. Johnny had treated him with respect.

He'd shown interest in him and paid him a great deal of
attention, joked, laughed with him. He loved Father's stories
about the Far East, and Johnny used to call him 'the Premier'
and be Anthony Eden, and Father loved it all. He'd never had
a son and he'd never been treated very well by his family
because we didn't like him. Johnny listened to his stories
about Singapore, Russia, the East Indies, Romania and New
York, all of the sea voyages he'd made. Father had still kept
his big brown leather travelling trunk, which was enor-
mously heavy, with hotel labels all over it. I remember only
one of them now, the Waldorf Astoria New York – the jewel
in the crown!

I remember when father was dying in hospital.

Jonnie, my nephew, had just been born, and I said,
'Jonnie's outside', meaning the little baby, not John Garley.
Father's face lit up and he said, 'Can I see him?' I didn't

realise, and I said, 'No, I'm afraid you can't; they won't let him in.' Johnny had died over three years before. I realised how deeply fond of him Father had been. The sort of son he would have loved to have had, bright, light-hearted, amusing, witty. One who talked to him, listened to him, respected him. Poor Father had missed out on that attention nearly all his life, and then he had felt the loss of it.

I didn't want to tell Father about Johnny dying because I felt it would upset him too much. But when I told my mother, she said something to me – mothers do, don't they?

I said, 'I'd left him to go . . .'

'You should never have left him.'

She was absolutely right I should never have left him.

But I was tired. I couldn't stand any more.

It was nonstop, because he couldn't sleep, couldn't eat, he talked all the time, he was obsessed.

I went upstairs again to see Father and talked to him for that one time – a long time – to talk about his own life. At the end he said, 'I thought no one understood', and he had tears in his eyes. My grief had opened me to compassion.

After Johnny died and I explained to his mother and his uncles, why I thought Johnny had done what he did, because of the guilt he had felt over his father and told them what Johnny had told me in his confession – the real facts. Theresa never spoke to her husband again, never wrote to him, completely disowned him. It hadn't been very helpful of me.

At the funeral his mother, clutching my hand as the coffin slid away through the doors into the back of the crematorium, said, 'He was my life.'

I'd felt it was very odd at the funeral when his family

seemed very cold and unfriendly to me but I had so many friends there that it didn't disturb me.

Outside the chapel, I stood in a daze shaking hands. As each one came up to me, I didn't know who they were. Their face, their name, meant nothing to me. After a blank moment, I realised that I knew who they were.

Going to look at the flowers for Johnny, there was a bouquet for me from Keith Michel, an old friend. I remembered then a play that Johnny had been in, *Flowers for the Living*.

I noticed a floral tribute in the shape of a pint pot, written on the card, 'From all at the Shakespeare.' It was for a publican. I showed it to Alan, 'Johnny would have died laughing'. Then realised what I'd said.

Everyone went to a pub and I went back to the hotel with Mrs Garley, Jack and Fred Garley, who was the middle brother of Johnny's father.

I realised why they had been strange with me: I had said to them, 'He gassed himself and I gave him the money', and they took it literally. What I'd meant was, 'No, I didn't, I only gave him the shilling for tea, hot water, washing up. You see, you have your gas supply on all the time, we have to put money in the meter.

'As for the eightpence, I left that for two calls from the phone box in case he needed me.' So then they understood that I hadn't given him the money in order to help him to kill himself.

Alan was very angry at Johnny for killing himself. He said to me, 'I felt like punching him when I saw him lying in the hospital in that brain-damaged state. "What a waste, you fool."'

We were all about to embark on a project together. Alan had been given the copyright of a play by the French playwright Marcel Achard, about two clowns which Alan and Johnny were going to play. We'd been working very hard to get a company together. We thought we had found a backer at one point.

Diana Churchill had said, 'I know a woman who's got money to give to the theatre'. Johnny and I went to see her and she promised that she would give us some money. Unfortunately this woman had cancer and it was all an illusion.

Johnny knew the Viscount Tony Furness, who'd succeeded his father at a very young age as his elder brother was killed in the war. Tony had seen Johnny playing Aumerle in *Richard II* at The Old Vic and because he himself was playing Aumerle at Eton he wrote to Johnny, saying he would be at a certain performance, and would like to meet him.

Johnny thought it was Georgie Rose playing a joke on him because it seemed so unlikely, but it was true. So they invited the Viscount to tea in their dressing room where their dresser brought in the tea, cucumber sandwiches and cake and made quite an occasion of it. And there they all were – Georgie Rose, Frankie Duncan, Johnny and the Viscount.

When Diana Churchill's source of money fell through, Johnny approached the Viscount to help in backing the company we were hoping to form. He invited us to dinner in a beautiful house in Eaton Square. A superb meal was served by the butler and there was a spotlit portrait of his mother Thelma, Lady Furness on the wall behind the head of the table. He said he was very interested and would like to have a meeting with Johnny and Alan Badel. This did finally happen but without Johnny and the Marcel Achard play was never performed as Alan didn't want to do it with any other actor.

I started rehearsals for *The Case of the Frightened Lady*, my TV play, the day after Johnny's funeral. Alan, Vonnie and I smoked our cigarettes and drank our innumerable cups of strong tea. We went for drives in the country and picnicked on the beach in Brighton, saw films and talked and talked and talked. On one of these drives, I saw what I thought was a UFO skimming a hedge, a long cigar-shaped object without wings – 'Look, look!' But it had disappeared. I knew what planes looked like, even in profile – I'd seen enough during the war: a Stuka dropping a bomb sideways on, a Messerschmitt machine-gunning head on, and we'd watched Spitfires in the sky overhead in dogfights performing their victory rolls when they'd shot down an enemy fighter, so I knew it wasn't a plane.

I can't emphasise enough the comfort that letters bring. I can remember sitting on the floor in Alan and Vonnie's flat, being so grateful. Drawing on those letters I received such a sense of their writer's love for Johnny and for me.

One often shies away from writing them, thinking one's words will be inadequate, but they won't be, not if they're written straight away before you have time for thought. I had almost a hunger for letters and they held me up when I read them.

You need only to hear the appreciation of the one who's gone and of how you were when you were together. I only remember one phrase that was written in Emlyn Williams's letter. 'How his face lightened up when you came into the room.' I cannot thank them all enough, and now so many are no longer alive.

I was with the hugely supportive Badels for three weeks and their generosity sustained me.

They were both very interesting to talk with, especially Alan, who had this fascinating mind which could interpret the meaning of a part and the intention of a play so well. For example, he saw *King Lear* in an unusual way for the time, as a summer play.

The heavy heat inflaming the passions of his daughters causing their irritability before the coming storm, their clothes that scarcely kept them warm, the high corn in the fields. In *The Merchant of Venice*, Portia's acceptance of Bassanio as her husband is full of allusions to money –

> *You see me, Lord Bassanio, where I stand*
> *Such as I am. Though for myself alone*
> *I would not be ambitious in my wish*
> *To wish myself much better, yet for you*
> *I would be trebled twenty times myself –*
> *A thousand times more fair, <u>ten thousand times more rich</u> –*
> *That only to stand <u>high in your account</u>*
> *I might in virtue, beauties, <u>livings</u>, friends*
> *<u>Exceed account.</u> But <u>the full sum</u> of me*
> *Is sum of nothing . . .*

Alan, whom Yvonne called Blade, an anagram of his name Badel, which accurately described him, kept my mind engaged with such imagination, like an archer shooting arrows in the air, and kept it away from thoughts of Johnny.

Once Alan understood the reasons which led to Johnny's suicide, he was empathetic. It had disappointed him greatly that Johnny and he wouldn't be acting together in the Marcel Achard play.

Later, I was asked to audition for the company. I didn't get the part. He was on holiday at the time and was aghast to learn of this on his return knowing that I had been so instrumental in helping to form that company.

Dear Alan and Vonnie I was to meet again when Vonnie was to look after my first baby Louise, for a day. She had a great time being slid down the back of the bath into the water with a splash. Their very talented actress daughter Sarah was fourteen when we met for the first time, I was pleased when Vonnie told me that she'd always liked me because I talked to her as if she were an adult.

Surrounded by friends, in the weeks following Johnny's death I was asked to stay by so many people. Tara Bassett, a dear student friend from the Vic days, invited me to stay at her parents' house in Winchester. Mark Dignam and his lovely wife, whom Denne Gilkes called 'the black-eyed marigold', a name that described her so accurately, her real name escapes me, invited me too, into their home.

I gave up the flat in Elsham Road; I never went back there except to get my belongings, which were few. The day I went back, I saw the gasmen checking the gas connections and emptying the meter. I said to one, 'Was there any money left in the meter?' And in the next breath I said, 'No. Don't tell me!'

I didn't want to know how much of my one shilling and eight pence had been used up. I didn't want to know whether he would still have been alive had I not left him the coins.

Epilogue

Having thanked the Badels for all their concern and kindness, I left them to take up their normal life again and went to stay with Judith Stott and Jeremy Burnham in their flat in Montagu Square.

I have never thought before about how this wave of kindness had swelled around me. It was better to stay with friends, as my family were mourning too. It's only now I realise the true loss of him to them, his infectious humour and his generous nature. We would not have been able to help each other through sadness.

Judith and Jeremy Burnham were perfect to be with in a completely different way. Jeremy played his guitar and sang the new Harry Belafonte songs to me, and he made me laugh in his light-hearted way. Judith was incredible; the household was run seamlessly, but with no sense of strain. We went to bed at eleven and rose at eight, bathed one after the other, breakfasted. Jeremy went about his business, Judith left notes for her cleaning woman – 'Would you polish the table with half vinegar and half water? Thank you' – and then attended to me: 'We must get something done about that black head' – she was looking critically at my hair. Off to Biagio's in Lansdowne Crescent, where I received the best haircut I've ever had, cut in such a way that it turned up naturally at the ends – no help from setting lotion, tongs or permanent wave.

'You need some new clothes, my darling. Best port of call C and A.' Or, our joke, in the French way 'Cee a tah!' – the one at Marble Arch, her favourite browsing clothes store. Jude, examining the clothes swiftly, moved to the back of the rack and that's when I had my embarrassing encounter. An actor was in front of me and I couldn't remember his name. He'd been at Stratford with Johnny and me, and I was hoping Jude wouldn't appear so that I wouldn't have to introduce her. He went, Jude reappeared, I told her and she said, 'I knew, my darling, that's why I hid.' It's odd how one's memory becomes faulty after a traumatic experience. Apparently, it's a defence mechanism to protect one from suffering the effects of it too vividly. The memory does return, but I still can't remember that actor's name.

It happened to me again, a year or so later. A friend and I were talking to another actor from that same time, and in the middle of the conversation I started a sentence and was about to say his name when suddenly I stopped and said, 'I'm sorry, I can't remember your name!' He looked quite taken aback, and my friend was appalled.

Jude and I would go on day trips to Brighton on the train, quicker than taking my beloved car, as she needed to be sure of being back for her evening performance. She was in a play, *The Chalk Garden*, at The Haymarket with Sir John Gielgud and had sat talking with him on the journeys on the tour. He was very fond of her, as she was very amusing, unselfconscious, not in the least bit tongue-tied. On leaving the station, we'd call at the shops on the way to the sea to collect a picnic, then lie flat on the beach, not speaking again until we were on our way back to London – a peaceful and heavenly time.

I was sleeping in a small room on the mezzanine floor, on the landing at the bottom of their flight of stairs; I'd lie in bed, reading Judith's *Now-A-Days* book of fairy tales. One night, coming into the house late, I thought I heard someone coming up the stairs behind me – nothing supernatural, just a man, maybe, who had no right to be in the house. So, having locked my door, I stood listening for any sound on the other side. Meanwhile, I pretended to talk to a supposed companion in the room, answering myself with low mutters from a non-existent half-awake man. I gave up after about ten minutes, realising I would be there all night, and called out of the window up to Jeremy and Jude's bedroom. He was down in a flash, with no complaint when it transpired my fear was unfounded.

Two weeks later, with my new haircut and new clothes, I left the calming effect of those two dear friends and went to Stratford-upon-Avon to stay with my best friend Stephanie Bidmead. Her husband Henry Barden had developed TB and was in hospital, so Stevie was on her own as well. With no fear of my intruding too long upon married privacy, I could have stayed longer than my usual fortnight, but I was to start work then at the Ipswich Rep. Henry being in hospital, I was sleeping alongside Stevie in their double bed, as I had with my sisters, and there we talked ourselves to sleep.

Derek Mayhen, who was one of our bridge four, was sharing a house at Stratford with Robert Arnold, and they and Stevie and I became a foursome – not a bridge four, as Bob didn't play. It was a beautiful summer and we spent our days outside in the warmth of the sun. One morning Stevie and I woke early, about six o'clock.

'Come on, Stevie, let's go and wake the boys and go for a swim.'

I drove us to Shottery, we threw stones at the windows of the old house where they had rooms, and we all went in search of a tributary of the Avon, to indulge my whim. We found a suitable one, and I was swimming happily when I became aware of a strong current pulling me downstream. What if I ended up in the weir on the Avon?

Bob was nearest to me and I called out, 'Quick, help me, I'm caught in the current!'

He reached out and grabbed my arm and hauled me to safety. He kept his body trim and strong, as we had been told we must do at the Old Vic School. He'd trained at RADA and was very much into health foods like black treacle, wheatgerm and whatever else was in vogue at the time. His strength and calmness were reassuring. He made me feel safe, and I think that is what drew me to him.

Back at Shottery, Stevie and I decided to breakfast with them. Bob had built a kitchen out of wooden boxes in one corner of his room, providing himself with shelves and cup-boards lacking doors – shades of things to come!

There was no milk. I said, 'I'll go and find a milk float, there's bound to be one about.'

Bob said, 'I'll come with you.'

I was sad to leave them all behind when rehearsals started in Ipswich. Driving at what had become my normal speed, very fast, often with tears streaming down my face, I was alone in the car for three hours. I was there with only my thoughts for company, as my new car had no radio; they would take me back to Johnny. I found it hard to be alone. Once in Ipswich, I was working in a good company of actors which is what I needed – most of us were in our twenties and early thirties and got on well together.

I was living amongst the family again, and grateful, as Rosebud and Lolo's friends were around to keep the house cheerful. It would be the last time I'd live at home, that year of 1957, until Rosie and I cleared the house after Mother died, five years later. I went occasionally to have supper with members of the company. I needed the companionship of actors: they are the best people to be with in troubled times – understanding and full of humour.

I had one strange experience, taking three of the actors to visit the well-known haunted house, Borley Rectory. They decided to climb over the wall into the gardens. I stayed in the car. Suddenly a shower of stones was thrown at my win-dows. Panicking, I put the car into first gear and started going backwards. But first gear went forward far left and reverse gear went backwards far right. It was impossible for it to be accidental. I started to scream, short, sharp, high-pitched shrieks. The others scrambled over the wall, into the car, I forced the car into first gear and drove off at breakneck speed.

'What is it, what happened?'

I answered them only with these screams for about five minutes. Finally I stopped the car and calmed down. Not much to tell, but we didn't go there again.

I left Ipswich after four months, when I was asked to be part of the chorus of *The Trojan Women* (or *The Women of Troy*) in a BBC production by the director Michael Elliott, who co-founded the Royal Exchange Theatre in Manchester. Casper Wrede and Michael had both been on the directors course at the Old Vic School. We used to ask Michael, 'What did Casper say?' as he was Finnish, and we didn't like to let Casper know we couldn't understand his accent.

I was rehearsing for this when I called in on Peter and Lesley Retey in Holland Street, whose basement Johnny and I had lived in for a while. Johnny's one-time caretaking job had required him to stoke a cranky boiler, which reminded me of Uncle Bill's behaviour when he couldn't get his Primus stove to light and mine when I had to clean the stair carpet down with a hand brush and dustpan. When I got there, there was a letter from Bernard Hepton inviting me to go for an interview for the Birmingham Repertory Theatre for their next season. That was serendipity, indeed, as I wasn't living with Peter and Lesley at the time, and the interview was to be on the following day; I wouldn't have got the letter in time if they'd forwarded it to Ipswich.

Bernard invited me to play Lady Macbeth and Hedda Gabler amongst other parts. I had no hesitation in accepting his offer. If I'd stayed on at Birmingham, the next season I'd have played Cleopatra – the only Shakespearean part I've ever really wanted to play. I was forced to withdraw, though, as by then I was about three months pregnant with Louise.

My destination then was Birmingham. I rented an old cottage, one of a row of four in the main street of Henley-in-Arden, halfway between Birmingham and Stratford and near to Stephanie and Bob.

Albert Finney was beginning to make his name at Birmingham, and only stayed for the first production, *Macbeth*, before he was whisked off to act in the West End by Charles Laughton and Oscar Lewenstein, who'd seen his first performance of *Macbeth*.

Unfortunately, my performance was dire for the first three weeks. Then I caught an awful cold and the part came alive for me – Doctor Greasepaint. We were extremely under-rehearsed. Albie had been studying it no doubt for weeks, as he'd had more time than I to do so because he was in the previous season. Bernard often cut the rehearsal short, saying, 'We won't do it again – it might spoil it!'

I'd been laughing with the stage manager before curtain-up, remarking, 'My first performance is going to be holding a candle in one hand and my nightdress in the other, avoiding tripping up all those steps and attempting to act a woman in torment.'

A prophecy of what was to come. I shouldn't have joked about it; it wasn't the sleep-walking scene that was my downfall, but the first scene of the play where the lady appears at the top of a flight of stairs reading a letter from her husband as she descends. I was seized by an unexpected fit of nerves that caused me to freeze. How the words came out is a miracle but they did, in a completely zombie-fashion. I felt as if I were an automaton.

I have never felt that since and I hope never to feel it again.

Eileen Atkins was in front: 'June you were wonderful!'

'You must be mad, I was appalling!'

She meant I *looked* wonderful. Poor Eileen, what a reception; I heard she dined out on it.

Stevie had been playing Audrey in *As You Like It* when she decided she was having a nervous breakdown, and installed herself in a psychiatric ward in Birmingham Hospital, removing herself after a week when she saw the condition of the other patients. During that week, the understudy of her part was off sick, and Eileen, who had been selling programmes out front of the Stratford Memorial Theatre, stepped in at very short notice, extremely successfully. This was her gateway to damehood, which she deserves; she is the strongest, most truthful actress I know. I worked with her fifteen years later at the Vaudeville in *The Provoked Wife*, both through Toby Robertson, and thought so then.

Eileen was helped on her way by Toby, who was an actor in the Stratford Company with her and became a director afterwards. He gave us constant work during the Sixties. He kept me working in both the Prospect Theatre Company and in many television plays for ten years during my early motherhood, and I owe him a very large debt. My career would have given up on me if it had not been for his generosity. He became personal friends of us both. I knew all his four children when they were small, rocking his son Josh in my arms – singing, 'Joshua, Joshua, sweeter than lemon squash you are!'

I saw a lot of Stevie during this season at Birmingham, and became close to Bob. When I was at the Ipswich Rep, I'd often driven to Stratford for the weekend to stay with Stevie, leaving Ipswich after the Saturday two shows to stay for Sunday, and drove back again at 6.30 a.m. to be at rehearsal for 9.30 a.m. I drove at my usual speed of 70 mph, the car's top speed – 82 mph if going downhill! – along two-way roads that were more like country lanes. To myself I'd say as I drove, 'You must stop driving like this, you'll have an accident.'

I saw a lot of Bob during my visits to Stevie, and had begun to write to him while I was away. Later, I found these open sheets of paper thrown haphazardly into the tops of the cupboards on either side of the fireplace in the house he shared with Derek, and was not pleased. It had not occurred to him that I might not want them read by anyone who happened to be around. He disliked gossip and writing, and never wrote to me at all.

After a while he started to stay with me in my cottage in Henley-in-Arden, riding over on his motorbike (it had a foreboding number plate ending in 666). When we ended up getting married on 5 April 1958, it was mainly because my landlady who lived two cottages away didn't approve of him staying with me. I think Bob would have been quite happy to live for ever in an engaged state, but I refused to 'get engaged' as I considered it a suburban notion. I wasn't pushing for marriage; I just didn't want an engagement.

We were married in the very old little church in Henley-in-Arden. All the company came to the wedding and reception, where we probably ate fried sprats and lemon meringue pie – my specialities at the time. The non-company guests were Rosie with her baby son Martin, who cried during the service and had to be taken out, so she missed most of it. They were staying with me in the spare room of the cottage. In a very conventional way, Bob had stayed in Stratford on the eve of the wedding. Derek said he was as nervous as a kitten as he set out with him for the start of his sentence.

The company guests rushed back to Birmingham after the wedding for the evening's performance. *The Teahouse of the August Moon* was playing at the theatre in which I appeared only as Japanese walk-on and wouldn't have been missed so they gave me the evening off. Bob had left Stratford by then and was rehearsing a part in a TV play, surrounded solely by nuns, so he was free. That evening, he became very twitchy and decided to leave to catch the bus to Stratford. Very concerned about this, I went off and joined him at the bus stop – so we disappeared, leaving Rosie and a sleeping Martin to amuse themselves. There was no radio in the cottage, but she was bound to find a book worth reading!

'Did she have to get married?' Mother's reply: 'We'll have to wait and see!' A question she was asked again when Rosie got married in Kensington register office. She must have been disappointed when Rosie hadn't, and also in my case: Louise was born nine months after the event, almost on the due date except for being a week early.

At the end of the season, Bob and I went to stay in Rosie and Leighton's flat in South Croydon as we had nowhere to live. We stayed in the attic, where there were three sparsely furnished rooms, and were joined by my embroidered felt rug and print armchair, and a big blanket in bright coloured squares that I'd acquired during the Birmingham season.

Once we were married, Bob never told me that he loved me. I would say to him, 'I love you', and his response would be, 'Do you? That's nice.' So I stopped saying it.

The whole process of having a family was a bit like opening the tumble drier and finding more clothes than you put in!

So I found myself having children – five in seven years, six if you include the baby that died. Louise, Sophie, William, Chloe and Naomi arrived one after another. Throughout all six pregnancies I kept working. I was onstage right up to the last week before having Louise, and back a month later – it never occurred to me to stop working.

There was only one problem with having all those children: I didn't have time to look after myself nor buy new clothes owing to our increasing financial demands.

I started off well, after the birth of Lulu, a month later I was playing at The Lyric, Hammersmith in *The Rough and Ready Lot* which was televised afterwards.

Then two plays at The Arts Theatre for our friend Toby Robertson – *The Lower Depths* and *The Buskers*. I took Lulu to rehearsals for this having fed, bathed and dressed her and got in the guard's van of the train to Charing Cross then wheeled her pram up St Martin's to the Arts Theatre. I also went on tour playing Lady Fanciful in *The Provoked Wife* which transferred to the Vaudeville Theatre.

Under the aegis of Toby Robertson, yet again, there were

many television plays, during which I started to be given 'below stairs' roles, I was always dying of some terrible disease or they'd have me playing an amusing lady in either North Country or Cockney accents. Once you get typecast in those roles it's very hard to find your way out of them.

Bob and I had separated for a while, my saying that I didn't want any maintenance as I'd earned a good salary for the two years before.

Then my work dried up. I was often disheartened.

This is the saga of my life, not as an actress but as the mother of five children who acted; someone whose ambition it had been to play leading parts in the London and the National theatres – Juliet, Ophelia, Portia, Lady Macbeth, Cleopatra – Shakespeare, Shaw, Strindberg, Ibsen, Chekov – culminating in a damehood for my brilliant performances!

The year before my being offered the part of Dot in *EastEnders* was my worst ever – things were getting desperate.

I had worked for only four plays in the whole year – two in the series *Relative Strangers* with Matthew Kelly playing the lead and me as the wife of Bernard Gallagher, one in Charles Dickens's *A Christmas Carol*, where I met Christopher Biggins, and one episode of *Minder* with Dennis Waterman and George Cole – all on TV.

My annual income had been £3,300 including the dole. When an electricity bill came in, I just didn't have the money to pay it. The electricity board suggested I pay it in instalments and I thought, 'What instalments?' I applied for supplementary benefit and they asked how much my two youngest daughters earned. They were in their first jobs and

I really didn't want to drag them into it. The others had left home.

We all thought in my day that being in a soap would, as we'd put it, 'ruin our careers'. By this time, after that disastrous year of thinking mine was on the slippery slope, I thought, 'What career?' Thankfully Leslie Grantham saw me in *Minder* and suggested me for Dot Cotton in *EastEnders*.

When I was offered a three-month contract by the BBC, with an option for a further three months, I gratefully accepted the chance of being in a 'soap'.

After eight years, in 1993 I decided that I wanted to do other things, so I produced and directed a play.

I did it all because I didn't want any other bugger telling me what to do! I took the play *Double D* to the Edinburgh Festival, the first play of the twenty-year-old playwright Matthew Westwood, with Anna Wilson-Jones, Samantha Giles and Charlotte Bellamy as the three girls, myself as the mother of one of them – a subsidiary part. During rehearsals we all rehearsed in a large flat I owned in Folkestone. With my daughter Louise as my assistant director to keep an eye on me when I was rehearsing my scenes and Sophie organising the logistics, we three doing the set design and buying the clothes and props. My cast-offs provided the furniture. Matthew chose the music. It was a wonderful time; I was in group theatre again. It was a very successful venture which transferred to The Kings Head, Islington. We were pipped at the post for Best Play on the Fringe by Jonathan Harvey's *Beautiful Thing*.

This production led to many jobs for me – one of them being *Absolute Hell* as Dame Judi Dench's sidekick at The

Royal National Theatre. At the end of four years, in 1997 having been asked to go back to *EastEnders* I returned, and I'm still there, taking time out to 'do other things'.

'Before honour is humility!'

My fate line rising from the mount of the Moon, the planet of dreams, romance and imagination at the lower outer edge of my palm, is to do with life being shaped by chance, not design – as in the case of a person with a driving ambition to succeed in becoming what they want to be, achieving a certain position in their chosen career and thus living the life that goes with it.

My sort of life brings with it insecurity leading to feelings of apprehension in later years. It's easier to be poor when you are young with all your hopes and dreams of success ahead of you.

Very fortunate it was for me that these expectations were realised two years short of my expected time of retirement, at fifty-eight. I was to become successful in a career in a way that had crept up on me sideways – but not in the way that I'd hoped for.

No classical kudos for me, I'm afraid, but doubly underlined success as a self-designated manageress of a launderette – and in a soap opera. The last thing I'd imagined! We must give thanks for all things, good or bad, so my faith informs me . . . !

To be continued . . . Should I live so long with most of my faculties.

'God willing,' as my granny would have said.

Acknowledgements

My thanks to my daughters, first and foremost Sophie who urged me to the starting line, with Louise and Naomi whipping me along ably assisted by Debbie, my dear daughter-in-law, who leaped into the saddle in an emergency, together with her daughters Hannah and Katie in their summer holidays, along with Mark Attwater and Carly (my editor), Jo and Abbie anxiously awaiting the results from the side-lines and Nigel, who took over the whip when I pulled up at the last fence and forced me to the finishing line. Not forgetting my son Bill for willingly lending me his wife and daughters and my other daughter Chloe for her Sunday evening visits, providing me with an oasis of peace, sympathy for my plight and her companionship.

I must thank my sisters, Rosie and Lois, who have shared memories with me from the past and have been neglected for the last two months, friends who constantly heard, 'I can't talk, I've got a deadline' – amongst them Barbara Windsor, Polly Perkins, Matthew Westwood, Enda Bardon (wife of Dot's Jim), Carolyn Weinstein, Jim, my PA for fan mail & friend, and Martin, my nephew, Princess Ashley from Florida, Andrew Silver from Boston and my faithful fans Johnny from Gosport and George from Poplar. I give thanks for all my marvellous friends, past and present, especially my dear friend Doreen Alexander and my maternal family after Micie died, who have kept me afloat throughout my life, with all its joy and woe.

P.S. I dread to think that I've left someone out. Please forgive me if I have.